Apostolos Papagiannopoulos

MONUMENTS
OF
THESSALONIKI

Rekos

Translation: Alkmini Paka
          Athina Dzoka
Printing correction: Hatzidaki Iren
Photographs: Nontas Stilianidis
Phototypesetting: Theodosis Georgiadis and Co.
Lay-Out, Cover design,Map of Monuments: Apostolos Papagiannopoulos.

On the cover: a representation of the city of Thessaloniki by the painter Aginor Asteriadis.

Published by John Rekos & Co
          P.O. Box 32.071,
          564 10 Stavroupolis Thessaloniki, Tel. (031) 696.587
Distributors: Athens, 15 Klisthenous str, Tel. (01) 32.51.564, 32.42.104
          Thessaloniki, 13 Ag. Mina str; Tel. (031) 271.063, 269.062
                    GREECE

Contents

A´ Historical Background

Thessaloniki, which is the second largest city in Greece today after Athens, has a long and compelling history. The city was founded 2,300 years ago in 315 B.C. by the Macedonian king *Kassandros*. This beautiful city, which is built in the shape of a horseshoe along the coast of the Thermaïkos Gulf of the Northern Aegean Sea, has always played an important role in Greek history.

It was considered to be the most important city of the Balkan Peninsula, a fact which proves what a wise decision and right choice of location Kassandros had made when he founded Thessaloniki.

Various archaeological excavations have established the fact that the area of Thessaloniki has been inhabited since at least as early as the beginning of the third millennium B.C. Finds of human settlements were discovered on man-made hills called *"Toumbes"* which surround Thessaloniki. Still, other arcaeological finds show that settlements dating back to the Iron Age (1000 B.C.) existed in the same area up until the 5th and 4th centuries B.C.

Small settlements called *"polismata"* grew in the areas surrounding the Gulf's natural harbour, the most important of these being *Thermi* from which the *Thermaïkos Gulf* got its name. This steady housing growth coincides in history with the expansion of the Macedonian Dynasty which made its way from the mountainous regions of Macedonia and the plains surrounding the rivers *(Ano) Aliakmon, Axios* and *Erygonas* towards the coastal regions of the Gulf, particularly during the reign of the Macedonian king *Amyntas I* (520-500 B.C.).

Prior to this, and as early as the 7th century B.C., a series of colonies was created in the Macedonian region, particularly in Halkidiki and along the Thermaïkos Gulf by Greeks who emigrated from the south, chiefly from the cities of Halkida, Corinth and Athens.

5

The *Macedonians* inhabited the northern region of Greece in around 2,000 B.C. They were Dorians who, unlike the majority of their people, did not continue their way into southern Greece but, remained and settled in the highlands of Macedonia instead. Basically, however, there were no differences between the Dorians who remained in the north and those who settled in the south as both spoke the same dialect, used Greek names and worshipped the same gods.

The 5th century ushered in a period of cultural greatness for both northern and southern Greece. Many cities such as Avdira, Thassos, Amphipolis, Olynthos, Pella, Dion, Aeges etc. were brought to their creative peak of expression in art and literature. Macedonia reached its height of glory during the reign of Philip II who became king in 358 B.C. at a time when Macedonia was on the eve of civil and external wars. After many long and arduous struggles, *king Philip* prevailed as the sovereign ruler of Greece, and particularly of Macedonia, at a time when the Greek city-states were in a state of deterioration. In later years, king Philip was to win recognition as the founder of the idea of a United Greek State.

In 334 B.C. Philip's son *Alexander the Great*, king of Macedonia and indisputably the sovereign of the whole Greece, led a campaign against the Persians of Asia Minor. Following Alexander the Great's death in Babylon in 323 B.C., a struggle for the succession of his vast empire began. *Kassandros*, the eldest son of *Antipater* who was a general of Alexander's armed forces, did not accompany Alexander on his expedition to Persia. He remained in Macedonia as a Commissioner of the Macedonian state. Later, after the *"Successors"* had assembled *Triparadiso* in Syria (321 B.C.) Antipater was given charge of the empire while Kassandros was appointed commander-in-chief of the cavalry in Asia.

Copper amphora found in Derveni, near Thessaloniki. End of 4th century B.C. (Archaeological Museum of Thessaloniki).

Gold-plated, bronze crater found in Derveni, near Thessaloniki (330 B.C.). It is one of the most important exhibits of the Archaeological Museum of Thessaloniki. The surface of this unique piece is covered with relief representations of Silenus and Menades encircling the divine couple of Dionysus and Ariadne.

However, when Antipater died in 319 B.C. naming General *Polysperhon* as his successor, Kassandros with the support of Ptolemeos, Antigonos, Lysemahos and Eumenis who were his allies, turned against the new leader. Alexander the Great's mother also took part in this struggle for the throne, giving her whole support to General Polysperhon. At the battle of *Pydna*, however, which took place between the two opposing sides, Kassandros defeated Polysperhon and sentenced Alexander's mother, *Olympiada*, to death. His decision however, stirred up a great deal of opposition in Macedonia where Alexander the Great's achievements had already become a legend. Owing to these developments and in order to win the support of the Macedonian aristocracy, he founded *Thessaloniki*, naming it after his wife who was also Alexander the Great's half-sister.

His decision to found Thessaloniki and make it the new capital of Macedonia hinged on his correct judgement about the unsuitability of the former Macedonian capital, *Pella*, because of its lack of natural fortification, its geographical position and its inaccessibility to the sea.

Thessaloniki was built around the ancient town of *Thermi* and incorporated 26 other small towns, *"polismata"*, of the area, which, according to the geographer Stravon, included *Apollonia, Halastra, Gariskos, Aenia* and *Kissos*. Kassandros built Thessaloniki with the prospect of making it the future *"Metropolis"* of Macedonia. As it turned out, Kassandros's decision to found Thessaloniki was completely justified, as it soon developed into the capital city of Macedonia owing to its geographical position and political significance. Not too long after its foundation, the city was fortified with walls.

7

Thirty years after its foundation, *Antigonos*, king of Macedonia, chose Thessaloniki as a stronghold from which he defended himself against the invader *Pyrros* king of Epirus.

A little later, in 279 B.C., a band of *Celtic* raiders was crushed outside the fortified walls. Indeed, it was during this battle that the king of Macedonia, *Ptolemeos*, was killed while bravely defending Thessaloniki.

During the Roman Period, Thessaloniki prospered and soon became the capital of a Roman province.

In 168 B.C., when *Perseus*, the last king of Macedonia was defeated at Pydna by the Romans under the leadership of the Consul *Aemilius Pavlos* and following the defeat of *Andriscos*, (148 B.C.) Macedonia became Roman territory. The whole Macedonia was then divided into four parts (*regiones*) and Thessaloniki became the capital of the *"second"* region of Macedonia («*Macedonia secunda*») for a period of twenty years.

It was during this period that many monuments and art treasures of Thessaloniki and Macedonia were transferred to Rome by Roman prefects or *"collectors"* and were displayed as trophies of their victory at festivals held to celebrate the Roman's triumph.

After 148 B.C. the four provinces were united to form one greater province known as *"Provincia Macedonia"* with Thessaloniki designated as its capital. Shortly thereafter, southern Greece was annexed into this larger province. This union was to last 120 years up until the time of Augustus (27 B.C.) when southern Greece was separated from "Provincia Macedonia" in order to form a new province called *"Provincia Achaïa"*.

During that period, Thessaloniki was considered to be the *"mother city of the whole of Macedonia"*. It was the most important city in the Aemos Peninsula not only owing to its prosperous economy and expanding industry but chiefly due to its great cultural and intellectual growth. The city was able to retain its Greek character, a fact which is proved by the numerous inscriptions and coins we have of that period. Thessaloniki's proximity to the military *"via Egnatia"* (Egnatia Street) was a definite advantage from which the city profited immensely. It was built by the Romans on the remnants of an earlier road, mention of which is made by *Aristotle*, in order to join the Adriatic (Dyrrahio) with Hellispont and Asia Minor. This major road which also greatly facilitated the transportation of goods is believed to have been located a few kilometres to the north of Thessaloniki.

However, it is not to be believed that the Roman legions which literally poured into Greece were always invincible. On numerous occasions during the first years of the Roman Occupation, Macedonia and Thessaloniki were imperiled by the threat of barbarous attacks. The Roman orator Cicero who, in 58 B.C., fled to Thessaloniki in exile speaks of the valour and fortitude with which the city's populace fought to rescue itself from one of these attacks by northern barbarians. In practically no time at all, fortifications were put up at the *Acropolis* of the *Ano Poli* where the people joined the Municipal Guard in an attempt to form a unity which would successfully thrust back those incessant invasions.

In 49-31 B.C. when the Roman Civil War broke out Macedonia was turned into a battleground for the two opposing forces (*those in favour of the Caesar* and *the democrats*). Thessaloniki offered its full support to the Imperial Army which was under the leadership of *Antony* and *Octavian* and in so doing placed itself in an extremely dangerous position should the opposition democratic forces prevail. However, the Imperial Forces triumphed at Philipi in 42 B.C. after which the people of Thessaloniki erected a triumphal arch at the west gate of Axios in honour of the two victors, Antony and Octavian who marched victoriously into the city.

As a result of this alliance, Thessaloniki gained the status of *"free-city"* («*Liberam Civitatem*») and was allowed special privileges, most important of which was the right to govern itself, a right which the city was to hold for centuries during the Byzantine Era. Proof of this newlygained privilege was that the city held free public meetings and its procurement of the full protection of the Municipal Guard. It was during this propitious period in the history of the city that Thessaloniki began to celebrate the *"Olympia"* and the *"Pythia"* games which were carried out in the spirit of the Olympic Games of their ancestors, while art and literature flourishing as never before. Famous scholars, writers, philosophers, poets and men of letters who lived and taught in Thessaloniki prepared the grounds for an even greater and more diversified cultural and intellectual renaissance which was aided by the rise in commerce bringing Thessaloniki in contact with other civilizations.

The favourable conditions that prevailed during the first half of the first century A.D. make it perfectly natural that the *Apostle Paul* has chosen Thessaloniki as his first station, after Philipi in his missionary journey throughout Europe in order to spread the teachings of Christianity.

During his sojourn in Thessaloniki in 50 A.D., St. Paul established the first Christian church which he characteristically named *"Golden Gate"*, the second Christian church in Europe.

A little later, Apostle Paul sent two *Epistles A´ and B´* which were adressed to the people of Thessaloniki and which today make up two of the most important Christian documents in existence.

During the Roman Period, Thessaloniki reached its peak of glory and achievement in the time of *Galerius* Caesar, Diocletian's brother-in-law and a member of the Roman *"Tetrarch"*. During his administration as governor of the Balkan Peninsula, or *"Illyricum"* as it was then called, he made Thessaloniki the seat of government (beginning of the fourth century A.D.). A magnificent palace was built then as well as big blocks of public buildings, many of which still stand today either in a complete or partial

Relief representation of the city of Thessaloniki ("Fortune" = Tyhe of Thessaloniki) from a marble arch found in the area of the Roman Palace, now in the city's archaeological Museum.

state of preservation (Rotonda, the Palace, the Triumphal Arch of Galerius, the Ancient Market place (Ancient Agora) etc. These monuments have come down to us as symbols of a grandiose period in the history of Thessaloniki.

Via Egnatia, a very broad street which corresponds to today's Egnatia Str. intersected the city. It extended from the *"Golden Gate"* (*Gate of Axios*, today's Democratia's Square) to the *"Kassandreotiki Gate"* (*Gate of Kalamaria* and today's Syntrivani Square). Another main road which corresponds to today's St. Demetriou Street ran parallel to *Via Egnatia* and joined the other two gates of the city, namely the *"Litea Gate"* which belonged to the western wall of the city and the *"New Golden Gate"* which lay to the east of the city. Yet another road, vertical this time, which may correspond to today's Venizelou Street, joined the harbour with the Acropolis (the Ano Poli) where the Municipal Guard of the city camped.

Furthermore, descriptions by ancient writers as well as various archaeological finds point to the existence of cemeteries in the eastern and western sections of Thessaloniki, outside the city walls in approximately the same location as those cemeteries of the Hellenistic Period.

In the beginning of the fourth century A.D, *St. Demetrius*, the patron saint and protector of Thessaloniki suffered martyrdom together with his friend Nestor . Henceforth, Thessaloniki was to become the centre of worship of St. Demetrius throughout the entire Christian world. St. Demetrius was inextricably associated with the fate of the city and the traditional belief is that on numerous occasions St. Demetrius intervened to save the city from barbarous attacks.

When the Roman Empire began to weaken, following the departures of Diocletian and Maximianus, *Constantine the Great* made Thessaloniki his base from which he waged a war against his brother-in-law Likinios (313 A.D.). In 324 A.D. *Constantine* and his army, which numbered 120,000 men, established themselves in Thessaloniki having first built a new and bigger harbour in the place of the old Roman harbour where he gathered his fleet of 200 triakontores galleons and 2,000 merchant ships, as is recorded by the historian Zosimos.

Having gained victory over his rivals, Constantine the Great became sole emperor. He founded the new capital of the Roman Empire, *Constantinople* or *New Rome* in the site of a former settlement of Megaris *Byzantium* in the Gulf of the Propontis. He then established Christianity as the official religion of the Empire. Hence forward, Constantinople and Thessaloniki were to become the two main poles around which the Byzantine Empire flourished for over one thousand years. Thessaloniki, "the second largest city of the Romans" and "the eye of Europe and primarily of Greece", co-ruled the Empire along with Constantinople which of course had complete dominion.

In the new period of history, Thessaloniki fortified its walls so as to be able to ward off incessant barbarous attacks. Great construction projects were undertaken during the reign of *Julius Paravatis* (361-363) and still greater accomplishments when *Theodosius* the Great took the throne (379-395). He chose Thessaloniki as his base from which to wage his wars against the Goths and other northern invaders. During his stay in Thessaloniki, he issued the order for 7,000 Thessalonians to be slaughtered at the *Hippodrome* and in this way took his vengeance on the inhabitants for rioting against the Gothic Guard and their leader Vouterihos (390 A.D.).

In the following centuries, from 395 to 695, Thessaloniki became the target of frequent invasions. The *Goths* of Alaric and Theodoric were successfully repelled as were the successive assaults of the *Slavs*, who came from the Carpathian Mountains, pushed southwards and constituted a veritable threat to the Byzantine Empire.

In 580, the *Avars*, a nomadic race from Asia, laid siege to Thessaloniki for two years. The city bravely resisted this attack.

During the whole of the seventh century, the city was once again endangered by the successive invasions and seiges of the Dragouvites, the Sagoudates, the Veleyezites, the Vaïounites and the Verzites. Thessaloniki was only relieved from these attacks when Justinian II, the Rinotmitos, defeated the Slavs and marched victoriously into the city with his troops in 688.

In the *"middle" years* of the Byzantine Empire (642-1071) Thessaloniki and Constantinople had joint-dominion over the Empire. Despite territorial restrictions, the Empire was now confined to the regions that had always been inhabited by the Greeks. Consequently, the Byzantine Empire took on a completely Greek nature.

It is not at all surprising therefore, that Thessaloniki had participated actively in all the Empire's chief events as can be witnessed by the great role it played in the great religious upheaval of the time known as the *Iconoclast's* Movement. It was during the reign of the Emperor Michael III when Thessaloniki had definitely established itself as a religious and philosophical centre that the two Thessalonian monks, *Cyril* and *Methodius* set off from Thessaloniki on a series of missions to Bulgaria, Syria, Moravia and to the land of the Hazari in order to spread the doctrines of Christianity. Their contribution to the cultural development of these people was indeed tremendous.

In 904, Thessaloniki was rounded by the Saracen Arab pirates at a time when the city was totally unprepared for military warfare. The city put up a brave resistance but was unable to escape defeat and for days it was mercilessly ravaged. The Byzantine historian, *John Kameniatis*, in his only written account of the capture of the city, describes in detail the cruelty and brutality of the Saracens who literally laid waste to the city.

Thessaloniki, however, survived these attacks but it was not long after the city had managed to regain its strength that another wave of barbarous attacks, this time the Bulgars, stormed the city. These attacks were to last over one hundred years (904-1065). Peace was restored thanks to the Emperor *Basil II* (976-1025) who, having Thessaloniki as his military base, defeated the Bulgars at Strimon in 1014. A period of peace and prosperity followed in the war-torn regions of Macedonia and Thessaloniki. It was during this trouble - free period that the popular religious festivals known as *"Dimitria"* began to be celebrated every October in honour of the patron saint of the city. Saint Dimitrius.

While these festivities were being carried on in an atmosphere of religious fervour, to the west of Thessaloniki in the vast plains of the Axios River, great commercial fairs were also taking place in which merchants from every corner of the Byzantine Empire took part, even from as far as Italy, Egypt, Spain, Phoenicia and the Black Sea.

Following the death of Basil II, the Byzantine Empire entered a state of decline and gradually began to weaken while external dangers abounded. At this time Thessaloniki confronted a new enemy, the Normans from Scandinavia who established themselves in various parts of Europe, particularly in Italy.

In 1185, the *Normans* or *Normani* armed with 80,000 men and equipped with 200 vessels laid seige to Thessaloniki by land and sea. The city, which was unable to obtain reinforcements from Constantinople fought a battle against odds and fell into the hands of its enemy, only to be once again brutally plundered. The Metropolitan *Efstathios* who fought on the side of his fellow citizens to save the city wrote a detailed *"chronicle"* about its capture and the looting and destruction that ensued. A few years later, in 1204, the Byzantine Empire was stormed by the Latin Crusaders of the west and Thessaloniki became the capital of the Frankish kingdom with *Boniface of Monferrat* as king. A new period of unprecedented oppression and subjugation began.

The capture of Thessaloniki by the Saracens (Arabs of the West). Detail from a miniature by Ioannis Skilidzis (Madrid, National Library).

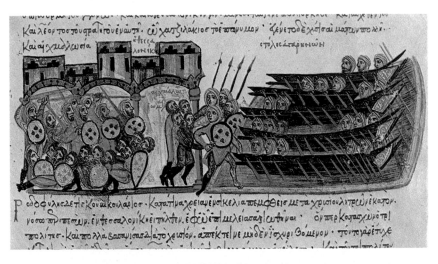

Latin reign lasted only twenty years in Thessaloniki. The despote of Epirus, *Theodore Angelos Comnenos*, after scrupulous military preparations and a series of wars reclaimed Thessaloniki and swore *"King and Emperor of the Romans"*. Thus was the Greek Empire of Thessaloniki created (1224-1246). Theodore fought to oust the Latins out of Constantinople and restore the Greek Byzantine State. Whatever the Comneni of Epirus failed to accomplish was at last achieved by Michael Paleologus, son of the then governor of Thessaloniki Comnenus Andronicus Paleologus. Michael ousted the king of Constantinople, Valdouino II and the Latin "Patriarch" Justinian, thus finally restoring the Byzantine Empire.

During the reign of the Emperor *Andronicus II* (1282-1328) Thessaloniki became the permanent residence of the Byzantine Queen Iolandi-Irene. Irene established friendly relations with the neighbouring Serbs. As a matter of fact, their leader *"krallis"* Stephanus Ouresi II Milioutin married the daughter of Andronicus and Irene, Princess Simonida (1299).

Unfortunately, it turned out to be a very short-lasting period of peace both for Thessaloniki and the surrounding areas. The threat this time came from the mercenaries of the Emperor, the *Catalans*. Having failed to conquer Constantinople, they turned their attention to Macedonia and Thessaloniki, looting and plundering every thing in sight. Even *Agio Oros* (Mount Athos) was not spared the enemy's ferocious attacks (1308). In the end, despite the seige by land and sea, Thessaloniki succeeded in repelling the Catalan invaders who were then forced to push onwards into Southern Greece, penetrating as far as Athens where they established a "Catalan" state.

Coin of the city of Thessaloniki from the time of the Latin Ruler Boniface of Monferat (1204-1207). After the establishment of the Frankish Rule in the Byzantine areas, the city became the seat of a Latin Kingdom (1204-1224).

During the Byzantine Period, Thessaloniki reached its peak of glory and prosperity in the fourteenth century which is rightly known as the *"Golden Age"* of the city. Despite civil strife, religious upheavals and social unrest which literally shook the Empire to its very core, Thessaloniki, for the most part a self-reliant city, enjoyed a period of fervent activity. The right to self-government which the city finally gained after long centuries of struggle provided an excellent background for the free development of Art and literature as well as for the promotion of commerce and industry. Celebrated scholars, orators, philosophers, mosaicists, craftsmen in wood carvings, hymnologists etc. — are closely associated with this "Golden Age" of Thessaloniki. *(Thomas Magistros, Nikolaos Kavasilas, Dimitrius* and *Prohoros Kydonis, Nikephoros Gregoras, Gregorios Akyndinos, Constantine Armenopoulos, Mathew Vlastaris, Nikephoros Houmnos, Manuel Panselinos* and others).·

Particularly in the areas of *church architecture*, hagiography and mosaic-making, Thessaloniki, in the fourteenth century, became a *"school"* for the whole Balkan region. Examples of this art which have come down to us, bear witness to this illustrious period in the city's history which is known as the *"Renaissance of the Paleologi"*. (Church of St. Catherine, church of the Holy Apostles, church of St. Nikolaos Orphanos, church of the Prophet Elias, church of St. Panteleimon, church of Taxiarhes, chapel of the Transfiguration of the Saviour, Vlatades Monastery).

During this period, Thessaloniki the *"populous"* and *"abounding in brave men"* city of the Byzantine Empire became the centre of a diversified religious and social culture which flourished in an atmosphere conducive to scientific inquiry, research and even social reform. In the religious domain, indicative of this favourable period was the Hesychastic Dispule which centered around questions concerning the very principles of the Christian Faith. The Hesychastic movement was led by *Gregorios Palamas* who later became the Metropolitan of Thessaloniki while those who opposed the movement gathered around the monk *Varlaam* who had come to Thessaloniki from Kalavria in southern Italy. The issue was to take on great dimensions even beyond the limits of the Byzantine Empire.

Of equal importance in the universal struggle for social reform and social justices was the well-known revolutionary movement of the *"Zealots"* which also took place in Thessaloniki. The *"Zealots"* succeeded in replacing the Feudal system in existence at the time with a popular Republic one that was to last seven years (1342-1349).

The Fourteenth century, however, was far from being a peaceful period in the history of Thessaloniki. The last fifty years were once again troubled by a long series of raids and new invasions at precisely a time when the Byzantine State was struggling to survive. The new enemy came from the depths of Asia — the *Ottoman Turks*.

During its long history, Thessaloniki suffered from numerous wars and continuous invasions of Slavs and other barbarians. The city faced these wars mainly with its own military forces which were sustained by the courage and decisiveness of its inhabitants. Here, a detail from a miniature, taken from a byzantine manuscript, showing warriors.

The *Turks* took advantage of the debility of the Byzantine State and the conflicts of the Balkan States. They gradually descended into Macedonia and the Balkan region, and then proceeded to put a tight squeeze rounol Thessaloniki. The city sank into a state of vassalage to the Turks under Murad I (1387) and was rescued from the clutches of its oppressors in 1403 when the former despot of Thessaloniki, *Manuel II Paleologus* became Emperor of Constantinople. When Thessaloniki was once again being threatened by the Turks, the despot of Thessaloniki, *Andronicus* together with the city's nobles yielded the city to the Venetians in 1423 on certain conditions which aimed at the city's rescue.

The *Venetian Occupation* of Thessaloniki soon turned out to be a new form of tyranny. The city's population, whose strength had greatly diminished, abandoned the city when instead it should have been preparing to confront the Turks and defend its autonomy. Consequently, the inevitable happened and in March 1430 Thessaloniki fell into the hands of the Turks of the Sultan Mourad II and a bleak period of oppression and subjugation began.

The Turks looted and came very near to completely destroying the city. Thessaloniki was literally deserted by its inhabitants while thousands of prisoners were led in chains and shackles to the slave markets of the East. The most important Byzantine churches were converted into mosques while still a large number of mansions were either confiscated by Turkish military officials or given to soldiers or other Turks who came to Thessaloniki with the prospect of profits to be gained through the war. Twenty-three years later, the Turks conquered Constantinople, an event of great historical significance as it exposed Central Europe and the entire Balkan region to the Turkish threat.

During the first years of the *Turkish Occupation*, the population of Thessaloniki was considerably reduced. Most of its population before and after the city's capture fled to the surrounding mountains of Olympus, Vermio, The Pieria, the Hasia, Pindos and Holomondas where they established refugee settlements. The sultan was then forced to take special measures to get the people, who had never given up hope for a better future, to return to the city. The Greek character was retained in many neighbourhoods while still new ones were created particularly within the proximity of small humble churches or monasteries which remained in the hands of the Christians (St. Minas, St. Theodora, Gregorios Palamas, Nea Panagia, Panagouda, Panagia Dexia, Ypapandi, Vlatades monastery etc...).

Gradually, the city began to recover its balance. The population began to increase steadily and Thessaloniki became a main port of the Ottoman Empire. Many travellers who visited Thessaloniki in the fifteenth and sixteenth centuries speak of their admirable impressions of the city (*Gio Maria degli Angiollelo* in 1470, *Joos van Christele* in 1481, *Pierre Bellon* in 1546, *Lorenzo Bernardo* in 1591).

Throughout the 15th century, succeeding waves of Jewish refugees, who had been expelled by the Christians of the western world, sought a home in the provinces of the Ottoman Empire. They were the *"Askenazim"*, Jews who came from Hungary, Germany and Bavaria and the *"Sefardim"* who were mainly from Spain. These Jews, who settled in Thessaloniki, established quite an important and active community and contributed immensely to the city's commercial life.

In the seventeenth century, Thessaloniki was a thickly-populated city. It became the seat of government for the Turkish *"santzàk-bèy"* and the *"mollà"*, i.e. a higher Turkish interpreter of the law and supreme judge. Thessaloniki was also the home of the Turkish commander («*kehayià-yerì*») and a vast army whose close vigilance virtually excluded any possibility of a civilian uprising.

The seventeenth century Turkish itinerant, *Evlià Tselepì*, in his *"Traveller's Guide"* has provided us with much valuable information about

Thessaloniki and its surrounding areas of this period. His description of the city constitutes a fascinating account of the lasting impressions he received of the many *"hamàm"* (Turkish bath houses), *"tarsi"* (market places) and *"Bozahanè"* (refreshment's stands). He viewed with great admiration the big multi-storey stone *"seràyia"* (mansions), the superb courtyards and public gardens. Equally impressive are the descriptions we have of the other Turkish itinerant, of the same century, *Hatzì-kalfà* as well as those of the European itinerants *R. De Dreux, Brown, Covel, Paul Lucas, P. Jean Baptiste Souciet* and *Felix-Beaujour* who visited the city at a later time.

The defeat of the Sultan Mohammed IV by the Poles and the Germans in the siege of Vienna (1683) definately marks the beginning of the decline of the Ottoman Empire while at the same time the first stirrings of a rebellion were obvious throughout the Balkan States. The Turkish yoke, however, became increasingly unbearable, particularly in Macedonia through which the Turkish troops had to pass on their way to the front or to areas where the people were forced to pay heavy taxes (*«avarìz»*) and suffered great abuse, humiliation and deprivation. In 1712, a plague resulting out of bad living conditions broke out and in 1713 over 8,000 people lost their lives. In 1720, the people of Thessaloniki were up in arms against their Turkish oppressors on the pretext that there was no wheat for bread. The same happened again in 1753, 1758 and 1789.

According to numerous descriptions of people who visited Thessaloniki in the 18th century, the city was at the time confined to the area within the byzantine walls, parts of which have remained in good condition. The areas around the city were yet to be inhabited. The city had four big Towers. Two of these towers, one circular, (today's *White Tower*) and the other square, were located at the southern part of the fortified walls. The population increased to approximately 40,000 people (Greeks, Turks, Jews). The streets in the commercial district were covered with boards which formed a roof (*«skepastà»*) which provided coolness in the summer. Another church of St. Demetrius was located near the seafront in the position of the present day Metropolis of Gregorios Palamas. Mention is also made of the churches of St. Athanasios, St. Nikolaos, St. Minas, Panagia and the crypt of St. Demetrius.

Macedonia and Thessaloniki contributed immensely to the struggle for *National Independence* of 1821. While Greek expatriates were negotiating the Greek issue abroad, civilians back home were sacrificing their lives and blood in their struggle for independence.

One of the most important members of *"Filiki Eteria"* was the armed partisan *Ioannis Farmakis* from Blatsi of Western Macedonia. Farmakis was awarded the title of "Leader of the Devoted". He set off from Constantinople in 1818, recruiting many notable personages from Macedonia and Thessaloniki to the cause for freedom. As a result of his efforts, quite an important revolutionary organization was formed in Thessaloniki whose members included *Hristodoulos Balanos, Athanasios Skandalidis, Stergios Polydoros, Kyriakos Tositsas, Argyro Tarpouhtzi, Anastasios Kydoniatis, Hrisanthos* and others. In 1820, *Ipatros*, another member of *"Filiki"* passed from Thessaloniki having in his possession letters and instructions from *Ypsilantis.*

When on March 23, 1821, *Emmanuel Pappas* from Serres declared open rebellion in Halkidiki against the Turks, the Turks in Thessaloniki vented their fury on the civilian population. At least 3,000 people, including the city's most important personages were massacred in the Turkish Municipal Building («*konàki*») and hundreds of revolutionaries were imprisoned in the White Tower.

The Turks promptly succeeded in putting down the numerous rebellions which had broken out all over Macedonia but the revolutionary spirit of the oppressed Greeks was not in the least bit daunted.

Towards the close of the nineteenth century, and while a free Greek state existed in the south, the Turks took big steps towards beautifying and updating their state which had fallen into a state of deterioration. In 1869, the Turkish governor issued an order for the demolition of whole sections of the Byzantine walls so as to create the impression of spaciousness. The first edifices to come down were the walls along the seafront and the big tower which was located near the port («*Yialoù-Kapoù*») at the height of the ancient *"Egyptian Market place"* (present day Egypt Str.). A few years later, the same was done to the walls of the armoury («*Tòp-Hanè*») and to the eastern wall which extended from the *"Kassandreotiki Gate"* (today's Syntrivani Square) to the *"Kanlì-Koulè"* tower (*Tower of Blood*) which, because of its formidable reputation as a prison, was painted white and renamed *"White Tower"* («*Beyàz-Kulè*»).

In 1867, a new road, the *"Sambrì-Pashà"* (present day Venizelou Str.) was built. Then, followed *"Midat Pashà"* (present day Saint Demetrius Str.) and in 1873 the *"Hamidiè"* Avenue (present day National Defence Str.) where all the Turkish administration buildings were built. In 1871, Turkey yielded to the pressure of the Great Powers of Europe and built a railway that connected Thessaloniki with Scopia. In 1888, Thessaloniki was united with Central Europe when its railway network was connected with that of Yugoslavia's. In 1893-1894, two new railway lines were built connecting Thessaloniki with Florina and Monastirion and finally in 1896, still another one connected Thessaloniki with Alexandroupolis.

Thanks to the mobility which the installation of the first horse-drawn "trams" brought in 1893, the city began to expand its limits and the first suburbs were created especially in the eastern section («*Exohes*" district). The overall appearance of the city began to change as imposing mansions or so-called *"pyrgi"* sprung up in the city's suburban areas. The city's population was by that time on a steady rise. In 1865 the population numbered 50,000 in 1880, 90,000 and finally in 1895, it increased to approximately 120,000.

By the beginning of the twentieth century, it was plainly evident that Turkish occupied territories in Europe would ultimately be restored to the people who had inhabited these areas for centuries. The decline in Turkey's domestic affairs had by then made itself manifest while at the same time the World Powers began to show an active interest in the region, a fact which greatly precipitated events. The civilian people's armed struggle served to bring out into the open the frequent interventions and ulterior motives of the Powers who wished to lay territorial claims to the Macedonian Region. Greece's struggle to defend its national integrity was given the name *"the Macedonian Struggle"* with the Greek Consulate (today's Museum of the Macedonian struggle) in Thessaloniki operating as its base. Although the people's struggle did not bring about immediate results, it did however contribute greatly to the liberation of the Macedonian Region and its final reinstatement into the Greek Nation.

On October 26th, on St. Dimitrius' Day and twenty days after the declaration of the First Balkan War, Thessaloniki was at long last liberated by the Greek armed forces.

B´ The monuments

The Walls

The city of Thessaloniki was walled in just after its foundation by the king of Macedonia Kassandros in 315 B.C. As we can assume from historical evidence king Antigonos chose Thessaloniki as the safest place from where to face the invading king of Epirus Pyrros in 285 B.C. Later, in 279 B.C. a band of Celtic invaders was crushed outside the walls of the city,

The plan of the city's byzantine ramparts.

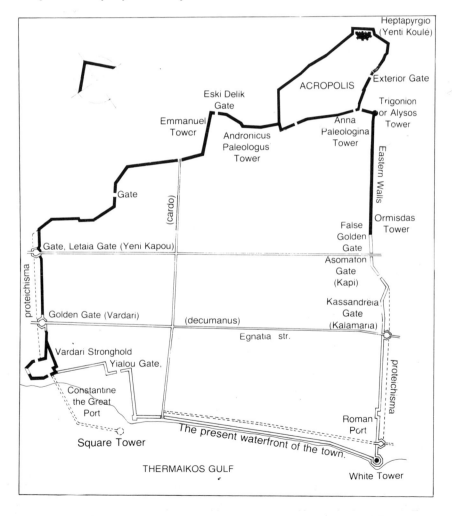

and notably in this battle the king of Macedonia Ptolemeos Keravnos was killed while he was defending the city.

Also, the walls saved Thessaloniki during the 1st century B.C. from barbarian Thracian tribes that laid siege to the city according to the testimony of the Roman orator Cicero, who lived in Thessaloniki in 58 B.C. after his exile from Rome. In order to confront this danger, the people of Thessaloniki were forced to construct hastily numerous new ramparts in the area of the *Acropolis*, in today's *"Ano Poli"* district and to repair also many parts of the pre-existing ones. Because of the city's impregnable fortifications the followers of Pompey and other senators took refuge in Thessaloniki during the civil war of the Romans since it was *"naturally and because of its walls well fortified"*.

During the Roman period there was no serious construction undertaking to the city's ramparts except for a few additions and repairs on certain parts which dated back to the Hellenistic period. The walls near the *Golden Gate* (today's Democracy Square) may have been underpinned when in 42 B.C. a triumphal arch was erected for the reception of the victors of the battle at Philippi Antonios and Octavios. There was similar undertaking, in the same area, during the 1st century, while in the east part of the walls, in the district called *Campos*, it is believed that Ceaser Galerius expanded the walled area of the city in order to construct his palacial residence (beginning of 4th century A.D.).

The ramparts of Thessaloniki were completed later through serious construction undertakings, mainly in the waterfront part, during the reign of Constantine the Great when he used the city as his military base in the war against his brother-in-law Likinios (324 A.D.). In order to face the danger of the frequent barbarian invasions, the emperor Julianos Paravatis ordered, during the same century, the restoration of Thessaloniki's walls.

During the reign of Theodosios the Great (379-395 A.D.), the most serious fortification undertakings started in Thessaloniki. Once again the city, became the temporary seat of the emperor, since it was geographically and stratigically appropriate, for the war against the Goths. An inscription that can still be seen on the east part of the walls refers to the activities of Emperor Theodosios who entrusted the Persian Ormisdas, an expert in the construction of fortifications, with the task of building the city's walls: *"by indestructible walls, Ormisdas completely fortified this town" (τείχεσιν ἀρρήκτοις 'Ορμίσδας ἐξετέλεσε τήνδε πόλιν...).*

Construction work continued on the walls of Thessaloniki during the reign of the Emperors Zenon (474-491), Anastasios I (491-518) and Leon the Wise (886-912). In 904 the Saracen Arabs captured Thessaloniki after having entered the city by means of the low walls which extended along the waterfront. As a result of this and in order to make the city safe, Emperor

View of the byzantine walls near the Acropolis. In the background, the tower of the Trigoniou (or of the Alesis = chain).

Romanos Lekapinos (919-945) raised the section of the walls which bordered the sea.

When the Emperor Vasilios II Voulgaroktonos (976-1025 A.D.) used the city as his seat during his wars against the Bulgarians he made several additions and restorations to the city's fortifications. However he neglected to reinforce the part of the eastern walls which remained most exposed to attacks from the sea. This vulnerable part of the walls was used by the Normans in order to enter Thessaloniki in 1185.

The tower of Trigoniou.   The tower of Manuel.

23

Part of Ormisda's inscription, on the city's eastern walls, opposite to the hospital of Agios Dimitrius, on todays Castron (= walls) Str.

Around 1230-1232 new construction work was undertaken at the northern ramparts at the Acropolis. It was at that time when the famous tower of Manuel Paleologus was built and where still exists the inscription saying: *"With the efforts of the mighty ruler Manuel this tower was built by Georgios Duke of Apokavkos with the efforts of Manuel our mighty ruler"* σθέν(ει) Μανουήλ τοῦ κρατίστου δεσπότου ἤγειρε τόνδε πύργον (αὐ) (σύν) τῷ τειχίῳ Γεώργιος δούξ 'Αποκαύκου ἐκ βάθρων σθέν(ει) Μανουήλ τοῦ κρατίστου (δεσπότου).

1. The inscription of Manuel on the northern wall (1230-1232).
2. The gate of Anna Paleologina in the eastern walls of the Acropolis (1355).
3. The inscription of Anna Paleologina on the gate with the same name (1355).

24

Later, during the 14th century while the city was threatened by the Katalans, the Serbs and the Turks, the reinforcements of the walls along the waterfront were completed by the military *"lawmaker"* (*«λογοθέτης»*) of the city *Ialeos* (1316). The republican government of the *"Zelotes"* (1342-1349) also attended to the fortifications of the city.

After the fall of the "Zelotes", the empress *Anna Paleologina* came to the city and supervised the reinforcement of the east part of the walls and also, the opening of the two new gates near the Acropolis. On the gate that stands near the tower of Trigoniou (or Alyssos) there is an inscription saying: *"This gate was erected by order of our mighty and holy Lady and Ruler Anna Paleologina, during the time when the wall's guard was Ioannis Hamaetos in ςωξγ indictionis Θ '''* (that is in 1355) *(ἀνηγέρθη ἡ παροῦσα πύλη ὁρισμῷ τῆς κραταιᾶς καὶ ἁγίας ἡμῶν κυρίας καὶ δεσποίνης κυρᾶς Ἄννης τῆς Παλαιολογίνας ὑπηρετήσαντος καστροφύλακος Ἰωάννου Χαμαετοῦ τῷ ςωξγ ἰνδικτιῶνος Θ '»)* (= 1355).

During the period of the Venetian Rule of the city (1423-1430) attempts were made to strengthen the city's defence system by the further reinforcement of the walls, while the Turks blockaded the city. The two towers as they still exist today, the *White Tower* near the waterfront and the tower of *Trigoniou*, are considered to be from that period.

Similar towers, smaller in size though, existed during the Byzantine period, all along the perimeter of the walls. These towers, that were called *"provoli"* had different shapes i.e.: square, polygonal, circular or semicircular and were 70 in number when the ramparts of the city had been completed.

The walls of Thessaloniki formed a four-sided shape, two sides of which ran perpendicular to the Waterfront side (eastern and western walls) and the other two, which where parallel to the waterfront (that of the

2.

3.

1. View of the Heptapyrgion complex, at the northern part of the Acropolis.
2. The southern (main) gate of Heptapyrgion. It is surrounded today by later additions that completely alter its functional character.
3. Built-in marble parapets, parts of marble columns and lintels as well as decorative brickwork are used as ornaments of the two pilasters in the southern (main) gate of Heptapyrgion.
4. Turkish inscription by Tsaous Bey over the southern gate of the Heptapyrgion (1431).

Acropolis on the hill and that which bordered the sea). They had an average height of 10-12 m. and a perimeter of approximately 8 km. long. Along most of their length, there was on their outside part another wall called *"the outer wall"*, or *"outer bastion"*, or *"peritihion"* (surrounding rampart) as it was called by the Byzantines. The two walls were intended to create "defense lines" against the invaders while on the outer area of those two fortifications and for a long period of time existed a ditch that was filled with water from the sea and had wooden bridges that were destroyed during the war periods.

The walls had approximately 4.60 m, of width, and are constructed of alternating rows of stone and bricks every 2-3 m that sometimes formed arches. The construction was better, near the gates, with the use of stone and marble corner-stones. There were also whole or broken statues and architectural parts from Hellenistic buildings, altars, or tomb-stones which were placed into the walls during their construction.

The most known gates of Thessaloniki's ramparts were: *"the gate of Rome"* (near the White Tower), *the gate of Kassandreotiki* (in today's Syntrivani Square), *"the Litea Gate"* (at the west end of St. Dimitrius Str.), *"the False Golden Gate"* (at the east end of St. Dimitrius Str.), *"the Golden Gate"* (near today's Democracy Square or Vardari) *"the Sea Side Gate"* (near the sea). Also known was the gate of Anna Paleologina that still exists in the "Ano Poli" near the tower of Trigoniou.

In the *Acropolis*, where the Byzantine guard of the city used to camp, there were 14 small gates that were called *"parapylia"* or *"paraportia"* (small doors next to the main ones) which were mainly for military use. Similar small gates existed at the waterfront part of the walls.

Until 1869 Thessaloniki was completely enclosed by its Byzantine ramparts. Immediately after that year a large part of the walls was demolished by the Turks in their attempt to embellish the city.

Built-in marble ionic capitals in the northern walls of the Heptapyrgion. Their use in the construction of the walls was not a result of shortage of building materials but of purely aesthetic considerations.

1. One of the seven towers of Heptapyrgion.
2. Eastern exterior gate of the Acropolis.
3. Typical detail of the construction system in the walls of the Heptapyrgion.
4. The White Tower.

4.

2. The Ancient Agora (The Roman Forum)

During the Hellenistic and the Roman period, the most important part in the city of Thessaloniki was the area of the *Ancient Agora*. Especially during the Roman period, the Agora (Forum) was the social and religious center of the whole town, where the most imposing and magnificent buildings were located.

The Romans, who were basically warlike people, borrowed many elements from the Greek architecture and urban planning. They applied the principles of Etruscan "right-angled" organization of space which provided a solution to the functional complexity that certain buildings presented.

During the Roman period and especially during the late imperial years, in Thessaloniki, as in every Roman province, the dominant functional and morphological elements were the standards taken from Rome.

Plan of the Ancient Agora showing the archaeological discoveries found to date. It is obvious that the complex extends beyond the limits of the excavated area, (north-west wards).

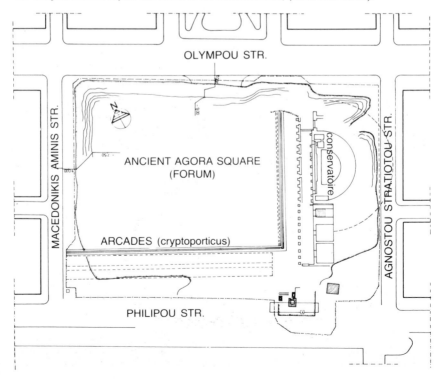

The main characteristic of the Roman town planning was the existence of two main axes that ran perpendicular to each other. The axis called *"cardo"*, pointed to a north-south direction and the second called *"decumanus"*, pointed east-west. These two streets were adorned with arches, peristyles and porticoes that usually formed open courtyards with springs, nympharms and fountains arround which the magnificent and sometimes pompous, public buildings were erected.

Archaeological research and certain historical evidence prove that a similar impression of splendour and grandeur was that given by the Roman city of Thessaloniki. The axis extending from north to south corresponds to the present day Venizelou str. that connected the port with the "Ano Poli" and the Acropolis, where the municipal guard used to camp. The other axis, is today's Egnatia str. (extending from east to west), that

View of the Ancient Agora area. In the foreground, the Conservatoire with its brick stand and the stage. To the left sections of the multi-storey gallery (cryptoporticus) and in the centre, the plaza.

31

connected the two major gates of the walls, that of Kassandreotiki, to the east and that of Axios to the west. In the middle of the present day Egnatia str., was the ancient Agora which corresponded to the Ancient Greek one following, though the model of the centre of Rome, the *"Forum Romanum"*.

The Roman Forum of Thessaloniki is supposed to have been built during the period 42-138 A.D. During these years many similar *"Agoras"* (*«Fora»*) were built in different Roman provinces. According to a different opinion the Ancient Agora of Thessaloniki was built during the period of the Roman *Tetrarchy* (end of the 3rd century and beginning of the 4th).

The Forum that lies between the streets: Philippou, Agnostou Stratiotou, Olympou, Makedonikis Amynis and north of Egnatia str., was discovered in 1966, during archaeological excavations. The results of these excavations were important for the study of the topography and history of the city. In the north-west part of the excavation area, a large rectangular space was discovered with traces of marble paving. Also a conservatoire was discovered in the east part of the same area with sections of the seats, part of which were constructed out of brick, and a part of the stage. Also, the ground floor of a multi-storey gallery (cryptoporticus) to the south, fragments of an arcade, mosaic floors, marble steps, a section of a stone-paved street, parts of sewers - pipes, many silver coins and stone statues, etc. An early christian fresco of great importance and value was also discovered on a wall's section of a gallery's compartment. This fresco represented two men in a position of prayer with a cross between them and Christ sitting on a throne, on the upper part of the painting. This fresco proves that the area of the Ancient Agora was used for the assembly of the Christians during the late Roman period and that this area is identical to the one which ancient writers refer to, in their narrations about the life and martyrdom of the city's protector, St. Dimitrius.

Stone paved street with smoothened limestone, at the southern part of the Ancient Agora.

1. A whole marble column and the bases of the arcade's columns that can still be seen near the conservatoire, give a picture of the organization of the Ancient Agora area.
2. Part of a mosaic floor in the arcade of the Ancient Agora.
3. Part of the multi-storey gallery (cryptoporticus) in the area of the Ancient Agora.

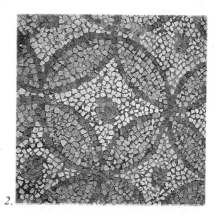

3. Rotonda

Rotonda is found north of Egnatia Str., in the eastern part of the old city and a small distance away from Kassandreotiki gate, today's Syntrivani Square. On the north-south axis of Rotonda, a small distance from it and next to the modern Egnatia str., there is still a part of *the triumphal arch (Kamara)* of Galerius with which Rotonda was directly connected, forming a single building complex.

Rotonda is one of the oldest and most important still existing buildings of the town. It was probably built during the years of the Roman *Tetrarchy* (end of 3rd and beginning of 4th century A.D.) and is one of the most important Roman buildings on an international scale. It was constructed exclusively out of brick, like the Triumphal Arch, the Roman Palace and the Octagon building in the area of the Roman Campos, in the eastern part of the city. It was probably part of the *"Galerian building complex"* that was built by Galerius during his sojourn in the city. Its functional purpose hasn't been determined yet. The prevailing opinion today is that it was used as an imperial mausoleum, while in the past it was believed to have been an idolatric temple dedicated to God *Kaviros*.

During the reign of Theodosios the Great (379-395) and after the baptizing of the Emperor by the Metropolitan of Thessaloniki Asholios, there were many alterations and additions to the monument in order to convert it into a christian church. One of the eight recesses was enlarged

Plan of the Rotonda. Part of the circular, peripheral, Theodosian aisle is shown here as well as later additions to the monument.

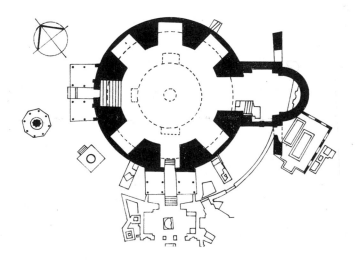

Northeast view of Rotonda. On the right the apse that was added to the monument during the reign of Theodosius the Great when Rotonda was converted into a christian church (379-395).

and extended eastwards in order to form the apse of the sanctuary. A new aisle was also added all around the building which had a width of 8 m and a lower roof, while the main entrance to the church was transferred from the southern side, where it was during the roman period, to the western in order to serve the needs created by the new christian religion.

The circular building of Rotonda consists of 8 recesses (including that of the apse) that have a width of 6.3 m. The impression given by the thick parts of the walls is more of piers than of wall sections. On top of each recess there is an arch and over each arch there is an arch-shaped window, while higher up at the bottom of the dome, there is another row of smaller windows.

The dome which is made of brick and has a diameter of 24.5 m, is not visible from the outside. The narrow peripheral wall is raised and covers the dome from the outside. The wooden roof of the monument, which is covered with tiles, rests on this wall.

The interior surfaces of the building were partly covered with colourful marble reventments and partly decorated with mosaics. Sections of these mosaics, still exist today on the dome and in the arches of the recesses. These represent saints from the first period of the Eastern Christian Church (Ananias, Romanos, Aristarhos, Cyril, Vasiliskos etc.) and other decorative themes (mainly in the arches).

These mosaics are supposed to be some of the most important of the early-christian period and equal in significance with those of Ravenna.

Taking into consideration evidence from the Metropolitan of Thessaloniki Efstathios (12th century) it is proven Rotonda was named *"church of the Asomati"* when it was converted into a christian church. Moreover, close to the building, at the eastern part of the walls, there was a gate called *"gate of the Asomati"*, from where the Normans entered the city in 1185. More recent excavations, however have taken place in 1983 along the east side of the Byzantine wall (to the north-east of Rotonda). These have changed the so far existing aspect about the place (or even the existence) of the "Asomati Gate" as no such findings were found there.

The *"church of the Asomati" (Rotonda)* served as the cathedral of Thessaloniki at least until the 13th century and maintained the same name during the period of the Ottoman rule (Eski mitropoli = old cathedral).

It has not been chronologically determined when exactly the church was named *Saint George*. The prevailing opinion is that, this happened after the erection of a small church of St. George to the west of the monument, where many valuable items and icons of the building were transferred when Rotonda was converted into a Moslem temple (*dzami*) in 1590 by the Turk Dervice Hortadzi - Souleiman (*Hortadzi - or Ortats - Souleiman Efendi-dzami).

Detail from the famous mosaics of Rotonda's dome. The figures represented are saints of the early christian age (Ananias, Romanos, Aristarhos etc.).

1.

South view of the Rotonda. The peripheral circular wall of the monument which is formed by three subsequent rings is raised up to the dome, which is covered by a tiled roof.

Part of Rotonda's dome mosaics. In the background behind the Saints figures there are representations of building complexes composed of edifices, arches and pediments.

2.

4. The Arch of Galerius (Kamara)

One of the most characteristic monuments of Thessaloniki is *the triumphal Arch of Galerius (Kamara)* which is found north of Egnatia str. and at a small distance from Rotonda.

"Kamara" is an edifice of the Roman *Tetrarchy* period (beginning of 4th century A.D.) and constitutes the western part of an arcade with arches. This triumphal arch was placed with its axis perpendicular to the old Egnatia str., — which intersected the town (from west to east) — and was part of the so called Galerian complex (Roman Palace) which developed towards the south in the area of today's Navarinou and Hippodromiou squares.

The Arch of Galerius was erected in order to honour the Roman Emperor when he returned to the city after his victory against the Persians (around 306 A.D.). The reliefs that can still be seen on the two remaining piers have themes relative to this event. These reliefs that are not distinguished for their exceptional artistic value — like most of the marble reliefs of this period — are organized in four horizontal zones. The top zone represents battles with cavalry and the Emperor Galerius entering the city on a horse, while crowds of people are welcoming him outside the walls of Thessaloniki. The next zone has as its central theme, battles of Romans and Persians while in the third one Galerius and Diokletian are shown while taking part in various rites. In the bottom zone, in a row of wall recesses there are representations of Nikes (Victories) holding trophies. The zones of the reliefs are separated by leaf-festoons, entwined garlands and flowers while in the upper part there is a cornice with decorative sculptured anthemia.

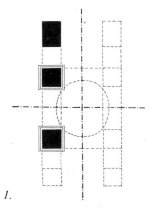

1.

1. **Plan of the Triumphal arch (Kamara) showing its two parts and the dome that rested on the central arches.**
2. **Eastern elevation of "Kamara".**
3. **Reliefs from the southern pier of "Kamara". Galerius and Diokletian are represented offering a sacrifice.**

2.

3.

According to archaeological evidence coming from excavations, "Kamara" was actually connected with Rotonda and also, in some way, with the Roman Palace that was to the south.

In Thessaloniki apart from the triumphal arch of Galerius there was also another one in the area of today's Democracy square (Vardari) which was also perpendicular to the axis of Egnatia str., near the gate of Axios (the Byzantine Golden Gate). That arch, which doesn't exist today, was erected by the people of Thessaloniki in order to honour the winners of the battle of Philipi, Antonios and Octavios (42 B.C.).

On the left: Galerius on a golden coin from the time of his reign (beginning of 4th century A.D.).
Below: the triumphal arch that once existed at the west end of Egnatia Str. It was erected in honour of the two winners in the battle at Philipi, Antonios and Octavios (42 B.D.).

5. Roman Palace – Hippodrome

Archaeological discoveries in the area at the *Roman palace* and *the Hippodrome*, within the walled in part of the city, give us a picture of Thessaloniki's splendour and flourishing state during the Roman period.

These arcaeological discoveries which were brought to light only two decades ago reveal an imposing building complex, the so called *"Galerian complex"*. It is almost definite that this building complex, that was erected during the period of the Roman *Tetrarchy* (297-307 A.D.) for the Roman Emperor Galerius, includes: *the palace, the Octagon* building, *the Hippodrome, the Arch of Galerius* (the processional street and the arch itself) and probably *Rotonda* as well.

From evidence coming from wall sections that were discovered in the area of the Roman Palace, we can conclude that this was an intricate building complex which had a dominant big open courtyard with a peristyle on its four sides. It is in this rectangular building — with its long corridors paved with marvelous mosaics of great value and of which many parts have been discovered — that one must search for the hall of the throne, the basilica for the assemblies and trials, the temples and rooms for the rites, the camps of the imperial guards, the dormitories, the mausoleums etc.. The traces of the fountains, the nymphaeum and the springs that were discovered, as well as the tow-storey gallery *(cryptoporticus)* located at the eastern part of the palace's site, can give an indication of the splendour of the imposing complex.

At the southwest part of the entire area, a big octagonal building was discovered, the *"Octagon building"* as it is called, whose function has not yet been determined. Maybe, it was the hall of the throne of Galerius' Palace, or the imperial mausoleum, or even a temple. The "Octagon building" has 7 recesses in its interior, with a big antichamber and circular rows of seats. The entire floor of this building, that had a diameter of approximately 30 m, was paved with marble stones forming an exceptional composition. A part of this paving and many examples of its interior decoration which still exist today can determine almost definately the relative aesthetic elements of the entire complex. Within the site of the building a whole marble arch was found with a span of 2.4 meters and with rich relief decoration. On the right side of the arch's front surface and within a circular frame there is a representation of the Roman Emperor Galerius (bust) while on the right side, and also within a circular frame, there is a representation of a woman's figure which is supposed to be the personification of the city of Thessaloniki. This arch, which is today at the Archaeological Museum of the city, has also representation of the God Dionysos and Pan.

Of equal importance were also the parts of the Roman *Hippodrome* that were discovered during excavations in today's Hippodromiou Square, to the east of the Roman Palace, and which extended as far as today's Tsimiski Str.

The *Roman Hippodrome (Circus)* was built similarly to the Ancient Greek ones, but it was longer, since it was used mainly for horse-races and chariot-races. So its length was usually 400-500 m. The Roman athletic games took place in stadiums (small or large) that usually combined thermae (public baths).

Sections of the eastern "long side" of the Roman Hippodrome in Thessaloniki were brought to light as well as remains of arches of the eastern part that were possibly used as entrances to the Hippodrome *(carceres)*. An inscription with the word «μονομάχου» (gladiator) on a clay little idol which was found in that area proves that Thessaloniki's Hippodrome was used for duel-fighting, a spectacle which the Romans were very fond of.

In the area of the Roman Hippodrome of Thessaloniki in 390 A.D., a big massacre of 7,000 citizens of the town took place after the command of Emperor Theodosios the Great when the people of the city revolted against the gothic imperial guards and killed their mercenery leader, Vouterihos.

At a certain historical critical moment, that has not yet been determined, the marble seat-rows of Thessaloniki Hippodrome were removed in order to be used for the urgent construction of some parts of the western wall near the Golden Gate in today's Democracy Square (Vardari).

Portrait of Caesar Galerius from a marble arch, found in the area of the Roman palace near the Octagon building (Archaeological Museum of Thessaloniki).

1. View of the Roman Palace. In the centre, the area of the courtyard (atrium).
2. Marble seats from the Hippodrome, that were used as construction material for the erection of the western part of the city's walls.

6. Christian Churches of Thessaloniki

6.1. St. Dimitrius

The church of *St. Dimitrius* is found almost in the centre of the old town of Thessaloniki, north-east of the Ancient Agora, and right next to today's St. Dimitrius Str., which follows the course of an older, pre-existing road of the city.

It is in plan a *five-aisled basilica* of the so called *hellenistic type* but has at the same time some special and rare elements in comparison to other churches of the same period in Greece. It is a timber-roofed building without a dome, and with dimensions in plan, 43.58 m in length and 33 m in width. The interior is divided into 5 aisles by four rows of marble columns (five aisled) while a sixth aisle is formed perpendicular to the others, where the apse is. The middle aisle (nave) which is wider than the other four and is raised higher, dominates the building's overall volume while the lateral aisles which are roofed separately and are lower, allow for the creation of different types of windows (single, double or multiple windows) in the lateral walls of the church.

The original walls are maintained in the largest part of the monument. The construction of the church is of stone and bricks that form beautifully shaped arches over the doors and windows.

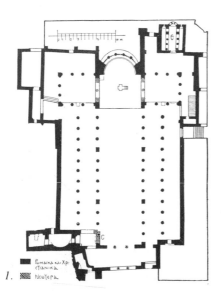

1. Plan of St. Dimitrius' church. On the left of the narthex, is the grave of Loukas Spantounis. On the top part of the plan, the apse and the chapel of St. Efthymios (13th - 14th century).

2. Western elevation of St. Dimitrius' church, Thessaloniki.

44

2.

When, in 324 A.D., Constantine the Great declared Christianity as the official religion of the Empire, the Christians of Thessaloniki hastened to honour their fellow-citizen and martyr, St. Dimitrius, and built a *small church («οἰκίσκος»)* on the site where — according to tradition — he had martyred and been burried. This site was near the underground ruins of the Roman baths and next to the *Stadium* of the city. After a small period of time, the small church of St. Dimitrius became a centre of worship not only for the city of Thessaloniki but for the entire Christian world. Christians came to Thessaloniki from all parts of the Empire in order to pray on the grave of the Saint, or to be cured from serious diseases by the myro (aromatic oil) that sprang from his grave. Among the worshippers was the ruler of Illyricum *Leondios* from Sirmio, who was cured completely of the disease he was suffering from. Then, Leondios out of gratitude to the Saint, built around 413 on the site of the small church an imposing church in honour of the Saint. This new building dominated the entire panoramic view of the city as it was built, at the foot of the slope towards the "Ano Poli". This was the church that survived through many alterations and additions until the big fire of 1917. The building then was destroyed almost completely but was reconstructed later according to its original plans.

45

The entrance to the church was from its west side, where once existed a big rectangular court with *peristyle (atrium)* and in its centre once stood a marble roofed basin where the worshippers used to wash their hands before entering the church.

At the north side of the church and right after the narthex there were three rooms, which were built in an earlier phase than the church itself and were probably parts of the old Roman baths near which, according to written evidence, St. Dimitrius was burried. It was in one of these small rooms and after the capture of the city by the Turks that the Saint's body was transferred in order to keep alive the tradition according to which this was the original tomb of St. Dimitrius.

According to written testimony, the corpse of the Saint was originally placed, *"underground"* (*«ὑπό τήν γῆν»*), at the left side of the nave and approximately in the middle of it, while on top of it a small hexagonal building was constructed, called "kivorio" and was made of silver and gold. The miraculous *"myro"* (aromatic oil) sprang from the larnax where his corpse had been placed. About this fact there is much written historical evidence. In the area of today's crypt, which is underneath the sanctuary, there was once the room with the basins where the holy oil was collected and which was at the same level with today's St. Nicolaos str., to the east of the church.

1. **Capital with cornice from a rectangular pier in the church of St. Dimitrius.**
2. **"Corinthian - like" capital from a marble column in the church of St. Dimitrius.**
3. **Representation of St. Dimitrius with two children. Mosaic from the northwestern pier of St. Dimitrius church. (17th century).**

1.

2.

3.

The church of St. Dimitrius was destroyed by a big fire between the years 629-634 during the reign of the Emperor Heraclios (610-641). Right after this, though, it was restored with few alterations and remained so until the fire of 1917.

In 904, when Thessaloniki was captured by the Saracen Arabs the church was plundered and the sacred "kivorio" of the Saint was dismantled and taken away, by the invaders. When the Normands, 281 years later, captured the city, in 1185, the new "kivorio" of St. Dimitrius' grave was again taken away.

In the 13th century, during the reign of the Emperor Michael VIII Paleologos (1261-1282), the church was restored and its wooden roof was replaced. The small chapel of *St. Efthymios,* in the eastern side of the church was also built during the period of the Paleologi. Its wall paintings were done in 1303 by order of the *«Protostratoras» (chief general)* and *Great «Stavlarhis» (stable-master)* Michael. According to a certain opinion, the wall paintings of this chapel are the work of the great hagiographer of Thessaloniki *Manuel Panselinos* who was the best known Greek painter of the middle ages and the main representative of the so called *"School of Macedonia"* during the period of Paleologi.

During the capture of the city by the Turks in 1430, the church of St. Dimitrius was plundered once more and even its walls were stripped bare according to written evidence of the Byzantine historian, Doukas. But the church, still remained in the hands of the christians for the next 60 years after the capture of the city by the Turks. In 1481 the marble rennaissance-style grave of the Thessalonean merchant *Spantounis* was placed in the interior of the church, to the left of the narthex. As it appears, Spantounis spent a lot of money for the preservation and restoration of the church.

The grave of Loukas Spandounis to the north of the narthex. This marble grave was placed in the church in 1481 in order to honour Spandounis, a citizen of Thessaloniki, and in return to his contributions for the restoration of the church.

1. The larnax in which St. Dimitrius' relics are now kept after they were brought back to Thessaloniki from the small Italian town of San Lorenzo in Campo.
2. The Altar of St. Dimitrius' church.

In 1490 (or in 1491) during the reign of the Sultan Vayazit II (1481-1512) the church of St. Dimitrius was converted by the Turks into a moslem temple (*dzami*) under the name *Kasimie Dzami* and remained as such until the liberation of the city in 1912.

The famous mosaics which decorated the church's interior walls in the Byzantine period were brought to light in 1907, during the period of the Ottoman Rule while the building was being restored. Most of these mosaics have St. Dimitrius as their theme and they were distinguished for their plain but at the same time, elegant technique of expression. Some of these mosaics were completely destroyed in the big fire of 1917 when the monument was almost ruined. Thanks to evidence that existed, the reconstruction of the church was made possible and was restored to its worshippers on October 26th, 1949, the day on which the memory of the protector of Thessaloniki was honoured.

The bones of St. Dimitrius are kept today in a special larnax in the interior of the church after being recently brought back from the Abbey of the small Italian village of St. Lorenzo in Campo. According to certain evidence the bones of St. Dimitrius were brought to this small village, during the middle ages by Christian monks and were burried under the Altar of St. Lorenzo's church.

49

View of the central aisle towards the sanctuary's apse of St. Dimitrius' church after the big fire of 1917.

St. Sergios. Mosaic from the west side of the apse's south west pier in St. Dimitrius' church. The delicate gradation of the colours and the overall structure of this picture are exceptional.

1. St. Dimitrius with a Deacon. Mosaic from the southwest pier of St. Dimitrius' church.
2. The offering of children to St. Dimitrius. Mosaic from the south aisle of St. Dimitrius' church.

6.2. Aheropeitos

The church of *Aheropeitos* is found in the centre of the old city of Thessaloniki, between the Agora and Rotonda, north of Egnatia Str.

It is a *timber roofed, three-aisled basilica of "hellenistic style"*, and is, together with St. Dimitrius and St. Sophia of Thessaloniki a typical *early christian church*.

The exterior of the building is of a simple and unpretentious style with its volumes organized in a symmetrical way on both sides of its axis which extends from east to west. The nave has dimensions of 37 m. in length and 15.5 m. in width and its roof is raised above those of the lateral aisles. *"Trilova"* and *"polylova"* (triple or multiple) windows which are formed along the raised parts of the nave's walls allow the light to enter and illuminate the interior space and the upper galleries of the church. Good interior lighting is a typical feature of that period's buildings (4th and 5th century, early christian period) during which christianity was adopted in the whole Roman Empire as the official religion and ideology.

Originally the church had at its west side an *exonarthex* of which only few parts still exist. Also it is certain that in front of the exonarthex and in the area of today's park of the Makedonomahi there was a square courtyard with *peristyle (atrium)* just like the church of St. Dimitrius.

In the interior of the church, the narthex was formed with its main axis perpendicular to the axis of the aisles, and was connected to the main church with three doors of which the central one was *"trivilos"* (triple) and

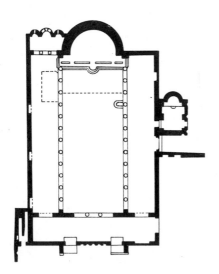

Plan of the basilica of Aheropeitos in Thessaloniki. In front of the narthex there are remainings of pre-existing structures from the exonarthex of the church which doesn't exist today. On the right, the small baptistry and in the top left corner of the plan, at the end of the north aisle, a small chapel.

originally shut with curtains (*«βῆλα»* - *vila*) as they are usually seen in Byzantine paintings.

The lateral aisles are separated from the nave by two rows of marble columns with Corinthian capitals decorated with acanthus leaves. On top of these two rows of columns and in the area of the upper galleries there are also two corresponding rows of columns.

The whole interior space, because of this composition, gives an air impression which is enhanced by the dazzling light that comes from the lateral windows of the building.

In the middle of the south aisle (outside the church) there is a small *chapel-baptistry*. Another similar one exists at the end of the north aisle, next to the sanctuary's apse which is the dominant architectural element of the entire eastern elevation of the monument.

The apse in the church of Aheropeitos. There are trilova (triple) windows on both sides of it. The small chapel of the church can also be seen in this picture, right next to the apse.

The exact time of the building's erection has not yet been accurately determined. The prevailing opinion is that the church was built right after the 3rd Oecumenical Synod of Ephessus, in 431, when Nestorios, who was considered to be an heretic, was condemned because he preached that the Virgin was not the *"mother of God" (Theotokos)* but simply the *"mother of Jesus Christ" (Christotokos)*. After this Synod, there were many churches built in honour of the Virgin in the whole Empire and most probably the church of Aheropeitos in Thessaloniki was one of them, named in the beginning *"Church of the Virgin, Mother of God, Aheropeitos* (not made by hands) *and Leading Lady"*. According to tradition the name Aheropeitos was given to the church because of a painting of the Virgin that was not created by human hands but had fallen from heaven. Moreover, it was supported by Byzantin writers that this painting was of the same value as the *"Aheropeitos"* (not made by hands) paintings of *"St. Mandilios"* and *"St. Keramios"*.

When the Turkish Sultan, Mourat II captured Thessaloniki and in order to impress that historical day on people's memory he ordered an inscription to be carved in one of the marble columns of the north row of columns which still can be seen, saying: *"The Sultan Murat captured Thessaloniki in 833 (= 1430)"*.

At some unknown time, during the period of the Ottoman rule, the church started to be called church of *St. Paraskevi*. So when the building was converted by the Turks into a moslem temple (*dzami*) it was named *"Eski Dzouma"* which means in Turkish; "old Paraskevi". According to the prevailing opinion the name "St. Paraskevi" was probably given to the whole area round the monument rather than the church itself, because there was supposed to be another church with this name, in that part of the city.

After the liberation of the city there were many restoration and reconstruction undertakings that needed to be done before the church was in condition to function again in 1930.

The small chapel-baptistry at the south side of the church.

1. Early christian mosaic from the inner surface of one of the arcade's arches in Aheropeitos church, Thessaloniki.
2. Mosaic floor that was discovered recently at the north-east part of the church.

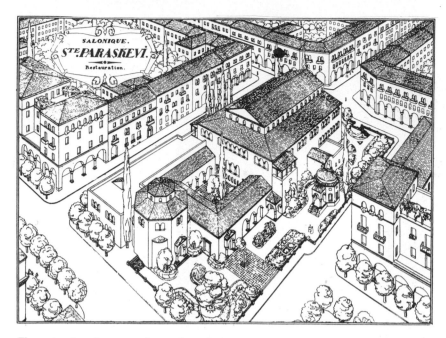

The restoration plans, according to the study the Aheropeitos church, in Thessaloniki, made by the French architect and urbanist Hébrard. The atrium and the west arcade that can be seen in this plan, do not exist today.

When Mourat the 2nd captured Thessaloniki (1430) and in order to preserve the memory of that historical day, ordered an inscription to be carved, in one of the north arcade's marble columns, which still can be seen, saying: "The Sultan Mourat captured Thessaloniki in 833 (= 1430).

6.3. Osios David (Monastery of Latomou)

The church of *Osios David* is found in the "Ano Poli" of Thessaloniki, south-west of the Vlatades Monastery.

This small church — that is probably a building of the end of the 5th century or of the beginning of the 6th — is a monument of tremendous historical and archaeological value — despite the alterations and additions that it suffered during the period of the Ottoman rule — since it is the "prodrome" of the *"cross shaped"* church with a dome which appears in a much later phase (second millennium). Originally the church was square with an apse to the east while in the inside it had four barrel vaults that were inscribed within the square, forming a cross. In the centre of the church, a square base was erected which was supported by the piers of the four other vaults. On top of this base a not perfectly shaped dome rested. Today a part of the original church (western) doesn't exist anymore. The dome was replaced by a tiled roof and the entrance to the church is now from its south side. These operations that had taken place during the Ottoman rule, when the church was converted into a moslem temple (*Soulidze or Keramentin Dzami*) have altered to a great extent this unique, cross shaped, early christian monument.

The name, *Monastery of Latomou* is due to the fact that, this small church was once the *"Katholikon"* of the so called Monastery that existed during the first years of the 9th century. It is said that this monastery was built by the daughter of the Emperor Maximianos Galerius, Theodora, who was secretely baptized christian by the archbishop of Thessaloniki Alexandros. When Galerius left Thessaloniki for one of his expedition Theodora transformed a bath-house, "valaneon", that was in the area that the Greeks called "Latomea" (quarry), into a *"sacred resort of God's Holy*

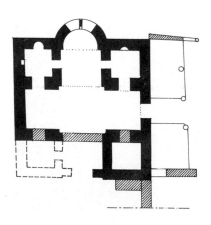

Plan of the, originally cross-plan, early-christian church of Osios David, in Thessaloniki.

57

Spirit" (christian church). According to tradition the only early christian mosaic inside the building, which represented Christ, was made after the command of Theodora herself, even though it is definete that this work was of a later phase (probably of the 5th century or the beginning of the 6th).

This mosaic which is placed in the apse, represents the *"vision"* of Prophet Ezekiel with Christ shown beardless, sitting on a colourful, illuminated arch. This work was covered with bovine skin in order to be saved during the Econoclast's movement and was discovered by chance during the reign of Emperor Leon Armenios (813-820). Since then and up until the Turkish occupation, the monastery had the name of *"Christ the Saviour"* most probably because of its famous mosaic's theme. During the period of the Ottoman Rule the mosaic was again plastered by the Turks and was discovered only in 1921. It was then, that its present name, *Osios David,* was given to the church, out of a necessity to honour *"the saint who practised in Thessaloniki".*

Besides its interesting architectural form and its famous mosaic, the church has also important frescoes from the 12th century, that are interesting and typical of the hagiographic art that flourished in Byzantine Thessaloniki.

Eastern elevation (with the apse) of the church of Osios David, Thessaloniki.

The famous mosaic in the apse in the church of Osios David, Thessaloniki.

The south (later) aisle of the church of Osios David in Thessaloniki. The monument has suffered many operations, mainly during the period of the Ottoman rule, that have widely altered its original plan.

6.4. St. Sophia

The church of *St. Sophia* of Thessaloniki is found south of Egnatia Str., towards the sea, a small distance from the church of Aheropeitos.

St. Sophia, together with the churches of Saint Dimitrius and Aheropeitos, are considered to be three of the most important early christian monuments of Greece and the Orthodox church in general.

The plan of the building can be characterized as a *domed basilica*. In particular, it is a building of a tranditional type from that of the *"domed basilica"* to that of the "cruciform domed" type of church.

St. Sophia of Thessaloniki, as well as the church of St. Sophia in Constantinople, were built in honour of Christ and the two buildings have many characteristics in common. The erection of the building started after the A´ Oecumenical Synod of Nicea, in 325, when Christ was aknowledged as the *"Divine Reason and Wisdom"*. There has been great discussion about the exact date of the erection of the building. It was maintained that the church was built during the same period as St. Sophia of Constantinople, during the reign of Justinian (527-565), and according to the plans of the architect Anthemios. It has also been attempted to determine the date of its erection by considering its architectural-morphological features, its building materials or the exceptional mosaics of its interior. The most prevailing assumption though, is that St. Sophia was built during the years of the *Econoclat's movement*, and most probably during the last quarter of the 8th century.

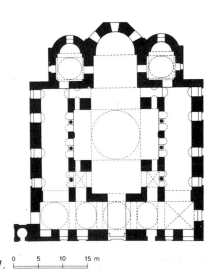

1.   0   5   10   15 m

1. Plan of St. Sophia's church, in Thessaloniki. The plan of the church is almost square in shape and is divided into 3 aisles by two rows of alternating columns and piers.
2. Eastern elevation (with the apse) of St. Sophia's church.

2.

The interior space is divided into 3 aisles by two rows of alternating columns and piers, while in succession to the lateral aisles, the narthex is formed, perpendicularly to the main axis of the building having as a result the almost square plan of the monument.

The dome of the church is encased on a square base, in the centre of the nave, that is formed by four crossed arches. This fact, along with other construction defects that can be observed in the composition and development of the volumes and the exterior surfaces of the building, prove that the church was built in a transitional period, during which the application of the cruciform domed plan, (which finally appears later in religious architecture), was still under development.

On the drum of the dome's base, which seems square from the outside, there are 12 windows over which and along the whole interior surface of the dome, the magnificent mosaic representation of Christ's Ascension, is recreated.

There is also another wonderful mosaic in the sanctuary's apse that represents the Virgin seated on a throne holding Christ in her arms, who is blessing with a gesture of his right hand. Notably, Christ's figure is of a later phase than the whole mosaic, and traces of an earlier mosaic cross, can still be seen, in the hands of the Virgin. The cross was replaced by Christ's figure when the period of the Econoclast's movement ended in the Byzantine Empire.

The church of St. Sophia was the cathedral of Thessaloniki from the time of Frankish rule (1204) until the time, it was converted into a mosque — after the conquest of the whole Empire by the Turks — under the name of *"Aya-Sophià Dzami"* and remained as such until the liberation of the city, in 1912.

The mosaic with the representation of Christ's ascension, from the dome of St. Sophia's church. Christ's figure is in the centre of the composition encircled by a multi-colour "dóxa" (glory). On the periphery of the dome's surface there are representations of the 12 Apostles with the Virgin Mary (9th century).

1.

3.

2.

1. Mosaic with Virgin Mary seated on a throne in the sanctuary's apse of St. Sophia's church, Thessaloniki (12th century).
2. West elevation of St. Sophia in Thessaloniki. On this side of the church there was a roofed arcade, traces of which are still preserved.
3. The central (west) entrance to the church of St. Sophia, in Thessaloniki.

6.5. Panagia Halkeon (St. Mary of the Coppersmiths)

The church of *"Panagia Halkeon"* is located in the centre of the old city of Thessaloniki, south-west of the Ancient Agora and north of Egnatia Str. It has a cruciform plan with a high drum-dome which is based on four crossed arches in the centre of the church. The construction of the building is exclusively made of brick which forms many decorative motifs, giving, in this way a certain elegance to the church while all the openings and arches are surrounded by straight or dogtooth brick stripes. When one takes into consideration its basic characteristics, *Panagia Halkeon* can be considered a representative example of the so-called *"architectural School of Constantinople"* and also an *"ancestor"* of the *"School of Macedonia"* where distinct solutions were given to the *"cruciform"* plan as for example in the churches of St. Panteleimon, Prophet Elias, Holy Apostles etc. Another unusual characteristic of the church is the existence of a second storey over the narthex, which is located on the west side of the building. Especially this element which is found in monastery churches, encourages the opinion according to which *Panagia Halkeon* was a monastery, but we don't have any evidence about this matter whatsoever.

The central dome rests on four pendatives that are supported by four monolithic columns whose capitals have a round base, are square on the top, and are decorated with relief foils and crosses.

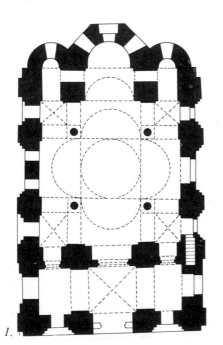

1. Plan of Panagia Halkeon church in Thessaloniki. Characteristic is the clarity of the arrangement of the building's parts, based on the cross formed by the four crossed barrel vaults.
2. South elevation of Panagia Halkeon church, Thessaloniki.

1.

On both sides of the apse, there are two small compartments that are directly connected to it, with two very low doors (these compartments are called prothesis and diakonikon).

In the centre of the church and towards its north side there is the tomb of its founder *Hristoforos* who was *"Protospatharios"* (royal dignitary) or *"Katepano"* (head) of *Lagouvardia*. What we know about the founder of the church comes from the inscription that is carved on the marble lintel of the west entrance and which is the following: *"This place profane until now, is dedicated, as a distinguished church, to the Mother of God by Hristoforos, the most famous royal protospatharios and head of Lagouvardia, and by his wife Maria in the month of September indictionis ιβ΄, in the year ϛφλζ (= 6537)"*. From this inscription we can assume that the church was built in 1028.

The words, *"this place, profane until now"*, indicate that the church was built on a site where once existed an ancient idolation temple, most probably dedicated to *Hephestos* and *Kaviros*, two gods that were connected to the art of coppersmithing, since according to tradition all the coppersmiths of the town were, and still are, gathered in that area. Also in the same site we can approximately locate the *"coppersmith's gallery"*, the *"refuge"* and the *"underground arches"* where Saint Dimitrius, the protector of the City of Thessaloniki, taught to the inhabitants.

The inner surfaces of the building's walls have interesting frescoes, which are considered to be contemporary with the church and which are: *"the Ascension of Christ" (on the dome), "the Last Supper" (in the sanctuary), "the day of judgement" (in the narthex) "the Pentecost", "Christ's birth", "the adoration of the Magi", the "Candlemas-day", the Crucifiction, the Assumption of Virgin Mary,* and others in different parts of the church.

During the Ottoman rule the church of *Panagia Halkeon* became a muslim temple (*dzami*). Its name was *Kazandzilar-Dzami* since it was located in the area of the coppersmiths that are called in Turkish *"kazandzidica"*.

1. The grave of the "head" (Katepano) of Lagouvardios Hristoforos, who was also the founder and sponsor of Panagia Halkeon, in the north aisle of the church.

2. Wall paintings from the apse in the church of Panagia Halkeon (1030-1040).

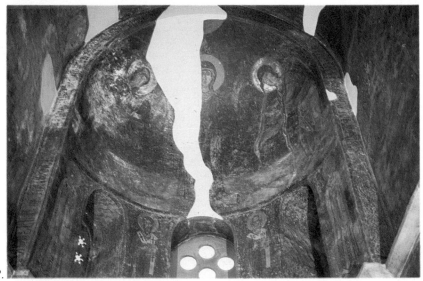

1. The grave of Hristoforos, founder of Panagia Halkeon church.
2. The Eucharist. Wall painting from the church of Panagia Halkeon (1030-1040).

6.6. St. Catherine

The church of *St. Catherine* is located in the north-west part of the old *"Ano Poli"* of Thessaloniki, north of St. Dimitrius Str. and near the Byzantine walls. It is a typical building of the so-called *"School of Macedonia"* since its plan is formed by four barrel vaults forming a cross, inscribed within a square, on which the central dome rests. This square base of the dome has an external aisle running along its northern, western and southern sides, which is lower in height and enlarges the interior space of the church while making it more elegant and morphologically interesting. On the four corners of this aisle, four domes are raised which are lower than the central one which remains dominant.

In terms of the arrangement of its parts and its morphology, St. Catherine's church has many common features with the church of the Holy Apostles of Thessaloniki, even though they are built in different periods (St. Catherine was built in the end of the 13th century, Holy Apostles, in the beginning of the 14th). Their similarities are apparent in their structural elements, as well as in the construction of the walls. Anyhow, the existence of these two monuments which have many common features, proves that in Thessaloniki, from the 11th to the 14th century, a considerable experience was gathered regarding the construction of churches that was passed to the Greek builders of the period of the Ottoman rule after, of course, getting adjusted to the new given conditions.

One of the main characteristics of the church, is the exceptional decorative brick work on its external wall-surfaces. The builders took advantage of every architectural and morphological element trying to enhance them by forming decorative brick rows around them. The wall paintings in the interior of the church are also interesting. They had been

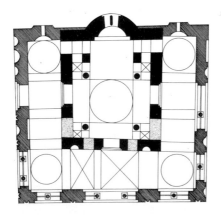

Plan of St. Catherine's church, Thessaloniki. The building's arrangement of spaces leads to the conclusion that the church is a typical example of the so called "school of Macedonia".

West elevation of St. Catherine's church, Thessaloniki. The arrangement of the volumes and the exceptional decorative brick construction of its walls are the two main characteristics of the church.

plastered by the Turks when the church was converted into a moslim temple (dzami) under the name of *"Yakoup Pasha Dzami"*. The frescoes, that are of the same period as the building, represent saints, scenes from the Godspel, Christ's miracles etc..

The frescoes of St. Catherine together with those of the other churches of the city — Prophet Elias, Holy Apostles, St. Nicolaos Orphanos, the chapel of St. Efthymios by St. Dimitrius church, St. Panteleimon, the small church of the Saviour etc. — prove that Thessaloniki was a centre of *Byzantine iconography* from where the art was spread to other regions of the Balkan peninsula. Certainly the small distance of Thessaloniki from *Mount Athos* as well as the relation and contacts with this monastic state contributed a lot to the promotion of the iconographic art.

1.

2.

1. Wall painting from St. Catherine's church, Thessaloniki.
2. Detail from the west elevation of St. Catherine's church with the elaborate brick construction system of the monument.

1. Detail from an exterior wall with built-in enameled tiles from St. Catherine's church, Thessaloniki.
2. Detail of wall construction system with incised marble parapets from early christian buildings, in the church of St. Catherine, Thessaloniki.
3. One more example of the elaborate brick construction of St. Catherine's walls in Thessaloniki.

6.7. Holy Apostles

The church of *Holy (or twelve) Apostles* is located to the south of St. Dimitrius Str., and it is almost adjacent to the west walls of the city and close to the *"Letea"* gate.

It is a cruciform church with dome, like St. Catherine, and belongs, in terms of its style, to the so-called "school of Macedonia" since the central dome rests on a square base which is formed by four crossed barrel vaults. As in St. Catherine, there is a lower aisle here, running along the three sides of the church (western northern, southern). On the four corners of this aisle, four domes are erected that are lower than the central one.

In the two ends of this aisle to the north and south, there are two small chapels, while on the right and left side of the apse, two alcoves are formed that are used for prothesis and diakonikon respectively.

On the western elevation there are six opennings, on both sides of the main entrance which are separated by four marble columns that have sculptured capitals, on which the semicircular arch of the façade, rests.

This monument apart from the exclusive aesthetic value of its morphology which is a result of both, the synthesis of its volumes and its architectural elements in particular, is also distinguished for its highly interesting and elaborate brickwork (its style is called *"plinthoperiktistos"*). Especially on its east side, where the apse is, wonderful decorative patterns are formed such as meanders, dogtooth stripes etc. that are evidence of a highly artistic building capacity.

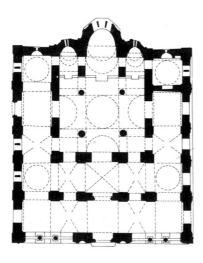

Plan of Holy Apostles church in Thessaloniki. As in all the Paleologian churches of the city the volumes of the building develop around 4 crossed barrel vaults.

The remainings of a vestibule and a masonry cistern that still exist on the north-west part of the building's site, prove that the church of the Holy Apostles was once the "Katholikon" of a monastery. The volume of the *cistern* (750 m³ approximately) can lead us to the assumption that the monastery had certainly been populous when it was at a flourishing state.

In the interior of the church there are notable frescoes and mosaics which are exclusive examples of the Paleologi period, (14th century) that were brought to light only in 1940 during restoration works. Here also the walls were plastered during the Ottoman rule when the church was turned into a moslem temple (*dzami*) under the name *"Soouk-sou dzami"*.

The exact year of the erection of the church comes from the monogram of the Patriarch *Nephon* that is incised on the lintel resting on the two columns of the narthex's apse. Another source of the church's date comes from an incised inscription of the south door's lintel (between 1312 and 1315).

North west elevation of the Holy Apostles church, Thessaloniki.

East elevation (with the apse) of Holy Apostles church, Thessaloniki. The morphology of the building and the composition of the volumes are very interesting as well as the elaborate brick construction of the walls with the beautiful decorative motifs and the dogtooth stripes.

1. Incised decorative piece from the portico of the Holy Apostles old Monastery, Thessaloniki. Part of this portico is found today on Paparigopoulou Str.
2. Ceramic decorations, with the monogram of the patriarch Nephon I, during whose patriarchy the Monastery of Holy Apostles was founded (1312-1315).
3. Sections of wall from the old monastery of the Holy Apostles that still stands today to the south of the church.
4. South elevation of the masonry water cistern of the Holy Apostles Monastery which still exists to the north west of the church.

1. The Transfiguration of Christ. Christ and the Prophets. Mosaics from Holy Apostles church, Thessaloniki.

2. St. Mathew. Mosaic from Holy Apostles church, Thessaloniki.

6.8. St. Nicolaos Orphanos

This small church of *St. Nicolaos Orphanos* is located at the end of St. Paul's str. and to the east of Herodotus str., south of Kallithea square of the old *"Ano Poli"* of Thessaloniki.

It is composed of a central raised part, and a roofed, Π-shaped, closed gallery that runs along its three sides (south, west and north). The central part which is the earliest one, is covered with a saddleback wooden roof, while the lateral parts of the "gallery" are covered with lean-to roofs. The central part is connected to the lateral and front aisles, with two double opennings (*«δίλοβος»-dilova*) to the north and to the south, and with a door to the west. The marble columns that are supporting, the double opennings, have interesting capitals of early-christian of *theodosian style*, with two rows of acanthus leaves. The central old part of the marble temple is extremely interesting. On both sides of the temple, at the east ends of the lateral aisles, there are two small chapels of which the north one is connected to the apse with a door and is used as *"prothesis"*.

The interior surfaces of the central aisle walls are covered with iconographic frescoes of exceptional artistic value that are considered to be contemporary with the building (14th century). These paintings possess a synthetic force, a rich variety of colours and have interesting themes. At the same time they compose a unique whole work of art since they are organized in a magnificent manner on the available surfaces and spaces. The organizing principle of these frescoes is the separation of this available space into three zones. In the lower one we find full-figure representations of saints, in the middle one there are only busts and on the top part whole scenes taken from the Lord's Passions and the Ressurection of Christ.

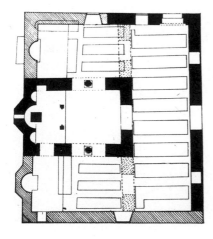

Plan of St. Nicolaos Orphanos church, Thessaloniki. The two distinctive entities of the plan, is the central part and the peripheral roofed arcade.

There are also interesting frescoes showing scenes from the life of St. Gerasimos and St. Nicolas, Virgin Mary, Saints' miracles, the office of the Virgin, and finally scenes from the book of the Monthly services.

The construction of the church's walls is also very interesting since there is an obvious difference in the technique and the construction materials of the central part's walls and those of the peripheral aisle. In the first case, the construction consists of alternating rows of brick and rough stone with different combinations and decorative motifs. On the contrary, in the case of the aisle, which is a later addition, there is a more simple construction system. Anyhow, the monument, in terms of construction, has many common features and similarities with the church of Vlatades Monastery, the church of Taxiarhes and the Holy Apostles of Thessaloniki. So, it is almost certain that the small church of Saint Nicolaos Orphanos is a building of the first half of the 14th century.

West elevation of St. Nicolaos Orphanos, Thessaloniki.

St. Nicolaos Orphanos belonged once to the Monastery of Vlatades and according to tradition, it was the church of a small monastery that maintained an orphanage. That was the reason why it was named St. Nicolaos of the Orphans. The prevailing opinion though, is that the church received its name from its founder who was called *"Orphanos"*. Inside the monument's courtyard and next to Herodotus Str., there are remainings of this small monastery's vestibule from where the entrance to the church still is.

Restoration of the original form, of St. Nicolaos Orphanos church, Thessaloniki, with the old portico of the monastery, remainings of which can still be seen right next to Herodotus str. (plan after A. Ksyngopoulos).

Parts of the old portico from the monastery of St. Nicolaos Orphanos, Thessaloniki.

1. Theodosian marble capital from the church of St. Nicolaos Orphanos, Thessaloniki.
2. East elevation (with the apse) of St. Nicolaos Orphanos church, Thessaloniki. In the picture, the difference between the construction system of the central part's walls and that of the peripheral aisle, is obvious.
3. St. Dimitrius. Wall painting from the church of St. Nicolaos Orphanos, Thessaloniki.

1.

2.

3.

1. Interior view of St. Nicolaos Orphanos church, Thessaloniki. In the foreground the marble temple of the church, further back the exceptional wall painting of the apse made during the 14th century.

2. The wedding at Cana. Wall painting from the church of St. Nicolaos Orphanos, Thessaloniki.

6.9. St. Panteleimon

The church of *St. Panteleimon* is found in the east part of the old city of Thessaloniki, west of Rotonda and very close to the arch of Galerius.

In this church for the first time, the characteristic features of the so called *"School of Macedonia"* are being finally formed. These are, the graphic dissimilar wall construction with bricks and stone, the contiguous decorative arches on the exterior surfaces of the building and the raising of the drums that create an obvious tendency upwards since on top of them the dome rests. The central dome, of St. Panteleimon church, is supported, first, by four barrel vaults that form a cross and then on four columns which stand very close to the exterior walls of the central part of the building, thus *"enlarging"* the interior space of the church. The dome of the narthex is placed on a lower level than the central one, an element that adds a special elegance and grace to the building.

Originally the church had an open aisle around its three sides (*«peristoon»*) that was destroyed later. The roof of this aisle was not supported by a continuous wall, as in the churches of St. Catherine and the Holy Apostles but on an arcade and on small sections of the walls. At the end of the northern and southern parts of the aisle there were two chapels.

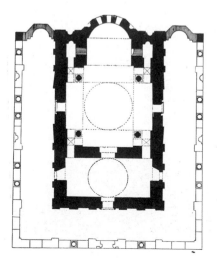

Plan of St. Panteleimon church, Thessaloniki. The placement of the columns, very close to the external walls is contributing to the widening of the monument's interior space.

By taking into consideration the structural elements of this church, its architectural morphology and its few, but of considerate value, wall paintings, we can assume that it belongs chronologically to the age of the Paleologi. From some manuscripts, that are supposed to be from the 14th century, we have evidence that St. Panteleimon was the *"Katholiko"* (main church) of the Monastery of Perivleptos or *"Lord Isaak"*.

After the conquest of the city by the Turks the church of St. Panteleimon was converted into a mosque under the name *"Isaakie Dzami"*.

South west view of St. Panteleimon church, Thessaloniki, after the earthquake of 1978 which severely damaged this unique, 14th century, monument.

Wall painting from the church of St. Panteleimon, Thessaloniki. The few wall paintings of the monument that still exist today are in the "prothesis" and the "diakonikon" and are contemporary with the church. (14th century).

6.10. Prophet Elias

The church of *Prophet Elias* is found at the north west part of the "Ano Poli" of Thessaloniki, between St. Dimitrius Str. and Athinas Str. (Olympiados), behind the building of the Ministry of Northern Greece.

It has a cruciform plan with dome and a square large narthex, called *"liti" (λιτή)*, according to the typical plan of the main churches (*Katholika*) in most Monasteries of Mount Athos. The central dome is supported, as in all churches of the same type, by four crossed barrel vaults. On the north and south side, of the sanctuary's apse there are two smaller ones that are called *"horoi"* and thus the plan of the church resembles in form a clover. This type of plan is called trifiloid or triconhos.

In the front - western part of the building, there is a square narthex, with four columns (*«liti»-«λιτή»*), which is connected to the main church with three openings and also to an upper storey by a built-in staircase. This upper gallery, that covers the whole area of the narthex, was used most probably for the storage of consecrated vessels or as a library.

Taking into consideration all the above mentioned features of the church of Pr. Elias, such as the existence of *"liti"*, of the *"horoi"* and the upper storey of the narthex, there is no doubt that the church was the *"Katholikon"* of a Monastery which was built after 1293 since that was the year when the first *"liti"* was built in Macedonia at the Monastery of

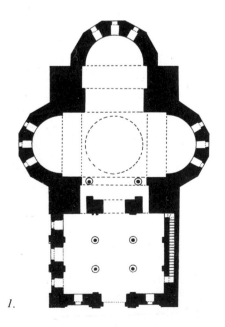

1. Plan of Prophet Elias church, Thessaloniki. The main characteristics of the monument are the "trifiloid" or clover-like shape which is formed by the apse and the two lateral apses (hori) and the existence of a four column square narthex which is usually found in monasteries (liti).
2. South west elevation of Prophet Elias church, Thessaloniki.

1.

Helandariou in Mount Athos. According to the prevailing opinion the church of Prophet Elias was the *"Katholikon"* of a Monastery that was called Nea Moni and which was built by Macarios Houmnos about 1360, on top of the ruins of the old Byzantine Palace.

There is much evidence supporting the opinion that this church was built on the site of the Byzantine palace of Thessaloniki. Through archaeological excavations that were done, on a small scale, in the area around the monument, it was proved that the foundations of the building were built partly on a rock and partly on the ruins of older edifices, of which many marble parts can still be found in the area around the church. This kind of foundation on two different materials is the main cause of the extensive damage that the building suffered with the passing of time. This fact made it essential for the building to be protected during the period of the Ottoman rule which was attempted by the construction of huge stone buttresses that were removed after the final restoration of the building.

The old *Byzantine Palace («Vasilia»)* of Thessaloniki, according to historical evidence, was destroyed during the big revolt of the *"Zelotes"* against the governor (*«protostratora»*) of Thessaloniki, Theodore, Synadino during the summer of 1342. The remembrance though of the palace, remained in the popular tradition, so when the Turks captured the city in 1430 they called the area around the church of Prophet Elias, *"Balaat"* which most probably is a distortion of the Greek word *«palati»* (palace).

2.

And morever, when they converted the church of Prophet Elias into a moslem temple (*dzami*) they called it *"Eski-Serai Dzami"* (= Dzami of the old palace) or *Sarali-Dzami*. Besides this, they also built, on the same site, the palace of the Turkish governor of the city, the *"konaki"*. And finally the governor's house that was built in 1891 was also located in the same area in order to follow the tradition according to which the area, around Prophet Elias, was distinguished and notable.

Besides its interesting architectural morphology and its elaborate brickwork (with contiguous arches and numerous decorative brick rows) the church has also interesting wall-paintings in the narthex that were, unfortunately, severely damaged during the time of the Ottoman Rule.

1. Detail from the wall of the south apse in the church of Prophet Elias, Thessaloniki.
2. South elevation of Prophet Elias church, Thessaloniki.

6.11. Vlatades Monastery

The *Vlatades Monastery* or (*Vlateai*) is found in the northern part of the old *"Ano Poli"* of Thessaloniki, south of the north part of the city's walls, opposite the tower of Paleologi and 130 m. above sea level.

The *Monastery of Vlatades* is the only one, of the numerous Byzantine monasteries of Thessaloniki that continues to exist until today despite the damage and destructions that it suffered. During the period of the Paleologi (1261-1453), Thessaloniki according to historical evidence had many monasteries (*«σηκῶν»-"sikon"*) within the frame of its walls and in the area around it. It was the time, when the Paleologi had shown great zeal for the invigoration of the people's religious faith that would contribute to the desirable unity which was essential for the facing of the serious dangers which were threatening to dissolve the Byzantine Empire. The Empress Anna Paleologina, showing great interest towards this direction, came and settled in Thessaloniki — following Catakouzinos' advice to her — in 1351 after the prevalence and triumph of the mystic sect of the *"Esyhastes"* that was led by the archbishop of Thessaloniki Grigorios Palamas. Together with Palamas the two monks *Dorotheos* and *Marcos Vlatis*, who belonged to the same sect, came to the city. They, according to the tradition, came from Crete, but were considered to be citizens of Thessaloniki. These two monks, that were distinguished for their education and their deep christian faith, founded around 1351-1371 the Monastery of Vlatades, and were probably assisted by Anna Paleologina, who, during the same period was restoring the part of the walls that was to the east of the Monastery's site. This new monastery, dedicated to *Pantocrator* (all-mighty) *Christ*, was honoured on the day of the Saviour's Transfiguration.

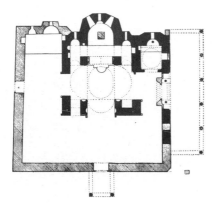

Plan of the Katholikon of the Vlatades Monastery, Thessaloniki. The black parts of the walls are sections of the original building (14th century).

From the old building complex of the Vlatades Monastery only few parts, still exist. Today's main church (*"Katholikon"*) is totally different, in form, from the original one which was built in the first half of the 14th century. The original parts of that building that still remain are: The sanctuary's apse, the chapel of the Apostles Peter and Paul, the dome and the walls around it, and the interior south wall. The remaining parts are from 1801, when the church was restored by a rich merchant from Thessaloniki called Ioannis Goutas Kaftantzoglou. The south arcade and the small vestibule of the west entrance were constructed in 1907.

The parts of the original church, which remained with the pseudo-pediments, of the dome, its alternating arches and the short columns at the corners, greatly resemble the church of the Holy Apostles (1312-1315) and generally it has many characteristics in common with the rest of Thessaloniki's churches of the period of Paleologi.

During the recent restoration works (1983) wall paintings of the 11th century were discovered in the "Katholikon" of the church which changes altogether the aspect that the building belongs, chronologically, to the 14th century.

The Katholikon of the Vlatades Monastery, Thessaloniki.

The way the dome rests on the sanctuary's walls and the south door-posts, without any columns, is architecturally interesting since that was a common feature of Greek churches between the 9th and 12th centuries. Anyhow the central part of the *"Katholikon"* is of a cruciform plan like the churches of St. Catherine and the Holy Apostles of Thessaloniki.

The wall paintings, that definetely existed prior to the capture of the city by the Turks (1430) as well as many marble parapets, icons and other unique valuable items that the Monastery possesses are extremely interesting.

1.

2.

1. Inscription from the west entrance to the Katholikon of the Vlatades Monastery. It refers to the restoration of the church during the year 1801. This restoration was made at the expenses of the wealthy merchant Ioannis Goutas Kaftantzoglou who was a citizen of Thessaloniki.
2. Inscription from the western entrance lintel of the Katholikon of the Vlatades Monastery, which refers to the recent restoration of the building in 1907. This restoration was made at the expenses of Sotirios Spyridon.

Besides the *"Katholikon"*, within the courtyard of the Monastery there are also: a) the abbey that was built in 1926 on the foundations of the pre-existing one, b) a recently built chapel dedicated to the Virgin, and c) the modern building complex of the Patriarchal Institute of Religious Studies. In the southwest part of the Monastery, under a rock, there still exists an ancient water *cistern* of the Monastery, where the water flowed through open and covered pipes from the springs of *"Hortiatis"* Mountain (*Hortaitis*), and was used as the main water supply of the city, from the time of the Byzantine period.

The *Vlatades Monastery* was a *"Stavropigiaki"* Monastery which means that was directly dependant to the Patriarchate of Constantinople. According to tradition, when the foundations of a new monastery were being laid, a cross would be placed on the construction site and that's where the term (stavros = a cross, pixato = to stick in) comes from.

During the period of the Ottoman rule the *Vlatades Monastery* was called *"Tsaous Monastir"*. The name probably came from the Turkish military governor "Tsaous Bey" who lived in the citadel, that was to the north of the Monastery, and who used to go there and enjoy the fresh air and the wonderful view.

1.

2.

1. The abbey of the Vlatades Monastery, Thessaloniki. This building was constructed in 1926 on the site of the monastery's old abbey.
2. The chapel of the Assumption of the Virgin. This recently built part of the monastery's complex is found to the west of the "Katholikon".

92

Restoration of the original form of the Vlatades Monastery (by A. Ksyngopoulos).

1.

1. Built-in byzantine plate in one of the walls of the "Katholikon" in the Monastery of Vlatades, Thessaloniki.
2. Marble inscription from the building complex of the Vlatades Monastery, Thessaloniki.

2.

6.12. Taxiarhes

The church of *Taxiarhes* is found in the northeast part of the old *"Ano Poli"* of Thessaloniki and south of Acropolis Str.

It is difficult today to determine the original plan of the monument since it has been greatly altered by later and recent additions. So while the church gives the impression of a three-aisled wooden-roofed basilica, it must have been originally a one-aisled church with a Π-shaped gallery on its three sides (northern, southern and western). At the south side, where once existed a roofed gallery a new aisle was added later, in order to enlarge the interior space of the church. There are still some visible traces of the way the parapets were supported and of the arcade's original railing on the three marble columns of the south front.

The results of a similar operation can be seen also on the west side — where the entrance is — with the addition of narthex. Here, as well it is possible that besides the exterior staircase with the two flights that led to the church there was also a roofed gallery.

The east part of the church ends in a five corner apse, seen from the outside, on both sides of which there are two small square compartments that are roofed with hemispherical roofs and where the *"prothesis"* (with a niche to the north) and the *"diakonikon"* (without niche, to the south). So the east elevation is not symmetrical, a feature that doesn't reduce the overall aesthetic value of the monument's composition.

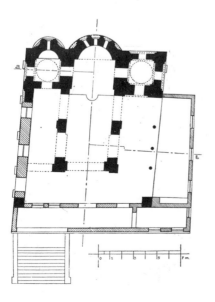

Plan of the church of Taxiarhes, Thessaloniki. The black parts of the walls are sections of the original building (14th century). The staircase and the western and southern roofed galleries, are later additions to the monument.

Beneath the floor of the church, which is considerably raised from the surrounding area, a "ground level" *crypt* is formed that resembles in plan the upper storey. Most probably this space with the numerous alcoves was used as charnel-house or for burials.

The church of *Taxiarhes*, from the exterior and in its original parts, presents the same construction system of all the 14th century churches of Thessaloniki (pilasters, dogtooth stripes and horizontal decorative patterns made of brick).

Taking into consideration all the morphological features and characteristics of the church we can assume that it is a building of the 14th century when the art of building churches flourished in Thessaloniki. Moreover the existence of the crypt-charnel house give a hint that the church might have been the *"Katholikon"* of a small unknown monastery that prospered during the same period.

The name of the church during the Byzantine period is not known. According to tradition, it was honoured on the day of the *two Archangels* and *Taxiarhes Michael and Gabriel.*

When the Turks converted it into a moslem temple (*dzami*) they built a minaret with two balconies which, as it is said, represented *the two Archangels.* For this reason the monument was called *"Iki Serife Dzami"* which means *"Dzami of the two balconies".*

Western elevation of the church of Taxiarhes, Thessaloniki.

In the interior of the building only few frescoes still exist: *"the Ascension"* in the east pediment and the *"Pentecost"* in the west one. These wall-paintings date back to the second half of the 14th century and are considered to be contemporary with the church.

Eastern elevation (with the apse) of Taxiarhes church, Thessaloniki.

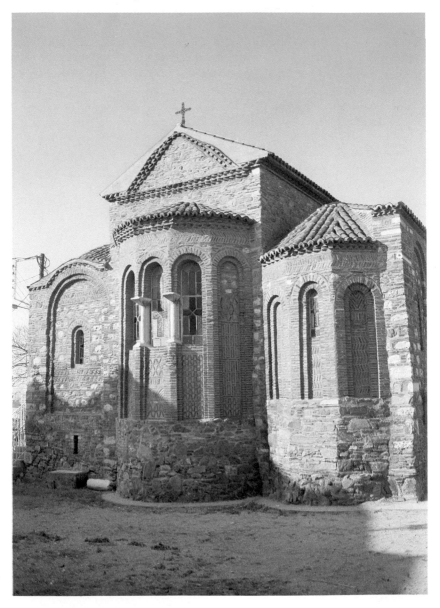

6.13. Transfiguration of the Saviour

The small church of *the Transfiguration of the Saviour* is situated alongside Egnatia Str. between the Ypapanti Church and the church of Panagouda and southwest of the Galerius Arch. It easily escapes notice not only due to its small dimensions but also due to the fact that the church's foundations are built at a much lower level than the surrounding buildings of the district. Nevertheless, it is one of the city's important monuments whose further research may uncover useful information of great archaeological and historical value.

Its architectural design is representative of the transitional period in the evolution of Christian church architecture, particularly of the Macedonian region. Its most outstanding feature is its tall and elegant dome which is supported by four *"blind"* arches which also make up the church's perimeter walls. Two small recesses, such as those found in monastic churches, were built within the thickness of the northern and southern walls of the church.

The chapel of the Transfiguration of the Saviour measures 5.5 by 6 square metres. A narthex, which communicates with the chapel by means of an opening in the wall of the western arch, was added at a later date (possibly in the sixteenth century) on the west side of the chapel:

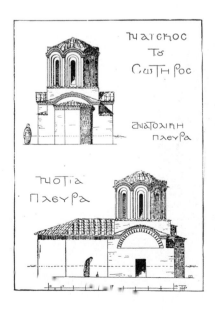

Eastern and southern elevation of the small church of the Transfiguration of the Saviour, Thessaloniki (14th century).

Of even greater interest than the wall structure itself is the dome which in proportion to the rest of the building is extremely tall.

The dome shares certain stylistic and ornamental features with the fourteenth century churches of Thessaloniki i.e. the semicircular pilasters and the dog-toothed rows, which can also be seen on the Church of the *Holy Apostles* and the *"Katholiko"* of the *Vlatades Monastery*.

Scholars believe the church was built in the first half of the fourteenth century during the age of the Paleologi. There is a lot of evidence to support the theory that this small church together with two other churches that were found in the area, were part of the historical Monastery of *"Lord-Joel"*. This monastery existed up until the sixteenth century at which time its grounds were "violated".

For a period of time, the church of *the Transfiguration of the Saviour* was dependant on the adjacent parish church of Panagouda which lies to the west a small distance away.

The earthquakes in 1978 caused tremendous damage to the church's dome which even prior to this had shifted from its vertical position. While the restorations of the dome were taking place, valuable murals contemporary to the church were uncovered.

The small church of the Transfiguration of the Saviour, Thessaloniki,

6.14. Saint Minas

The church of *Saint Minas* is situated in the southwest section of the old city, near the city's port and in the commercial centre.

Existing evidence supports the view that at the current site of this later dated church stood yet another very imposing eighth century church which was completely destroyed by a series of fires which broke out in the commercial centre of the city. Reference to this earlier structure which was the Katholiko of a monastery is made by a fifteenth century *inventory-taker* of the city.

Itinerants and historiographers make mention of at least five fires which destroyed Saint Minas. In 1770 and then again in 1818 and 1839 it was almost completely destroyed.

In 1890, however, the centre of Thessaloniki was devoured by flames and the church was reduced to ashes. In fact, the fires were so numerous that the Turks named the district of *Saint Minas "Yianik monastir mahalé"* which means the neighbourhood of the burnt monastery.

According to various sources, up until the beginning of the nineteenth century, the church of Saint Minas was modelled in the shape of the letter-T and was surrounded on three sides by an open arcade (*"Prodrome"*) and its impressive dome was visible even from the sea.

Western elevation of St. Minas church, Thessaloniki. In the background the elaborate bell-tower.

The church underwent extensive repairs in 1806 by the Thessalonian merchant Ioannis Kaftantzoglou who showed a deep interest in the restoration of the "Katholiko" of the *Vlatades Monastery* as well.

A short time after its destruction in 1890 the church of *Saint Minas* was rebuilt on the basis of an entirely different architectural plan. Two columns as well as several fragments of the marble sculptures which decorated the earlier church survived the fire and were incorporated into the new building.

A brief history of the church's reconstruction following the fire of 1839, is incised on the marble lintel above the western entrance of the church. In so far as the rapidly changing appearance of the city is concerned, of even greater significance is the fact that St. Minas is located within the building block which constitutes the last remaining part of the city's earlier urban scheme.

After the liberation of Thessaloniki, in 1912, it was in the church of St. Minas that the incident was celebrated with a magnificent service.

Detail from the western elevation of St. Minas church, Thessaloniki.

Interior view of the decoration of the dome in St. Minas church, Thessaloniki.

1.

1. Marble inscription over the western arcade in the church of St. Minas, Thessaloniki.
2. Inscription over the western (main) entrance of St. Minas church, Thessaloniki. This inscription refers to the disastrous fire in the year 1839 and to the complete reconstruction of this new church.

2.

6.15. Panagia Lagoudiani (Laodigitria)

The church of *"Panagia Lagoudiani"* (or *"Lagoudatou"*) is situated in the northeast section of the old city between Kassandrou and Athenas Streets.

This church, which during the Byzantine Period was the "Katholiko" of a convent received its name from its owner *Lagoudiato* (or *Lagoudato*) who is believed to have lived during the fourteenth century. *"Panagia Lagoudiani"* was directly dependant on the *Vlatades Monastery* which was founded at an earlier time by the Vlatades brothers (Vlati) who were monks.

Tradition tells us that the church of *"Panagia Lagoudiani"* derived its name from an incident involving a hare (*"Lagos"* means hare). The hare running to escape the pursuit of its hunter scurried down into a hole where the miracle performing icon of *"Panagia Oglaïtisa"* (or *"Triherousa"*) lay hidden. Of course this incident led to the discovery of the hidden icon and as a result *"Panagia Lagoudiani"* was built there. During the Turkish Occupation the monastery of Panagia Lagoudiani was called by the Turks *"Taousàn monastìr"* i.e. the monastery of hares.

The present Katholikon of Panagia Lagoudiani's female monastery, in the northeast part of the old town of Thessaloniki. The original building suffered numerous alterations and was finally rebuilt in the beginning of the 19th century.

During the hard times of the Turkish Occupation, apart from the nun's cells and the church itself, the surrounding areas were inhabited by homeless Christians from Thessaloniki whom the monastery provided with accomodation based on a rental system called *"itzarè"*. This meant that a Christian could secure a home by first depositing a lump sum of money followed by life-long nominal instalments. In this way, the monastery was able to retain ownership of its land whose sale was prohibited. These dwellings exceeded the number of twenty.

The church of *Panagia* has always had the name of *"Laodigitria"* though an explanation has never been offered as to the origin of this name. Many historians, however have associated the name of *"lao-odigitria"* (leader of the people) with an old Byzantine church, mention of which is made in the 12th century by Efstathios, the Metropolitan of Thessaloniki (*"the all pure Mother of God (Theotokos) who leads us"*). Indeed, *"Odigitria"* was considered to be the female patron of the city along with St. Dimitrius.

A part from an old map of the Panagia Lagoudiani area where it is apparent how the neighbouring area is related to the monastery.

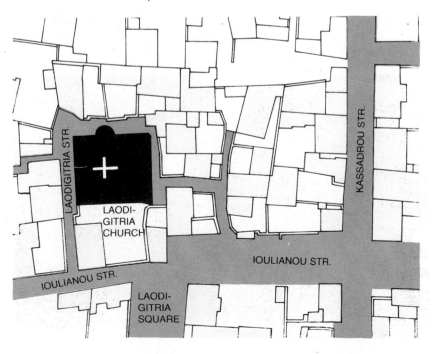

6.16. Ypapanti – Candlemas: (a religious festival, on February 2nd in honour of the presentation of the infant Jesus in the temple and the purification of the Virgin Mary).

This church is situated in the eastern part of the old city, alongside and south of Egnatia Street and east of the small church of the *Transfiguration of the Saviour.*

It is a later-dated building which, though of no architectural interest, is nevertheless of great historical significance since historians believe that up until the sixteenth century there stood in the area the *"Lord-Joel"* monastery mention of which is made in the patriarchal documents of 1520, 1542 and 1546.

It seems that during the Turkish Occupation, the present day church underwent such extreme renovations that its appearance was radically altered. Through close inspection of the small chapel of the Transfiguration of the Saviour, which possibly belonged to the monastery, we can safely conclude that the original church which stood possibly in the same position was as magnificent and vast as the monastery itself.

Reference to the present day church of *Ypapanti*, around which developed the major Greek residential districts during the Turkish Occupation, is made — in a synodal document of 1766 — by Samuel Hatzarìs, the Patriarch of Constantinople from 1763 to 1768. This document stated that the churches of St. Athanasios, Panagia-Lagoudiani, Saint Nicolaos Orphanos, Saint Ypatius (the earlier Panagia Dexia) and the church of *Ypapanti* were not dependant on the Patriarchate of Constantinople but on the Metropolitan of Thessaloniki.

1.

1. North elevation of the church of Ypapanti, Thessaloniki. Most of the incised marble stones in this building's walls are considered to be parts of the byzantine gate of Kassandreotiki which once stood to the east of the church, on today's (Syntrivani) = Fountain Square.
2. Partial view of the church of Ypapanti. The construction system of its walls is interesting as the plaster is covering part of the construction materials (system of "Hidden bricks"). Also in this picture are shown some of the marble incised pieces in the church's walls, which come from earlier buildings of the monument's area.
3. Inscription from the north entrance to the church of Ypapanti.
4. Stone arch from the church of Ypapanti, Thessaloniki.

2.

3.

4.

6.17. Saint Georgios

This small church is located west of and near Rotonda, on the street once known as Apostolou Pavlou.

This church belongs to a later period and is of no architectural interest. It was once the *"Katholiko"* of a small monastery which originally belonged to the Metropolis of Thessaloniki but was handed over, in 1700, to the *Monastery of Gregorios* in Agio Oros (Mount Athos). In 1758, when Gabriel was Metropolitan of Thessaloniki, the church itself was also given to the Gregorios Monastery in a state of partial ruin due to severe neglect. In 1815, it was completely renovated.

Tradition tells us that in 1591, following the capture of Thessaloniki by the Turks and the conversion of the Church of *the Asomati* (*Rotonda*) into a moslem mosque (dzami), the Christians of Thessaloniki, needing a place to transfer their valuable heirlooms and icons, built the church of *Saint Georgios*.

East elevation of the small church of St. Georgios, Thessaloniki. The building is located opposite to Rotonda's west entrance.

6.18. Panagouda

The church of *"Panagouda"* (or *"Mikri Panagia"*) is situated south of and alongside Egnatia Street and west of the chapel of the Transfiguration of the Saviour near the old *"Greek High School"*, a building which has survived to the present day.

The earliest written reference we have of the church is a codex dated 1789 in which the accounts (katastihon) of the church were kept. It reads «ἐν Θεσσαλονίκῃ ἐκκλησίας τοῦ Γενεσίου τῆς Θεοτόκου ἐπονομαζομένης Παναγούδας» *i.e. Thessaloniki, Church of the Birth of the Virgin Mary also named Panagouda.* This codex is presently being kept in the National Library of Athens.

In 1817, the church was completely destroyed by fire and a number of valuable heirlooms, ecclesiastical books and icons were lost. However, a splendid fourteenth century *«epitaphios»* was salvaged and is now being kept in the Byzantine Museum of Athens.

The church of *Panagouda* was rebuilt in 1819, in the same year that the churches of Saint Constantine (at the Hippodrome which was demolished), Saint Athanasios, Nea Panagia (Megali Panagia) and Saint Ypatius (Panagia Dexia which was also demolished) were also reconstructed.

Prior to 1789 and during the Turkish occupation, the church of *Panagouda* existed as a *"metohi"* or part of the property of Agio Oros (Mount Athos). For a period of time, the small church of the Transfiguration of the Saviour, which lies to the east, existed under the authority of the church of *Panagouda.*

Indeed, itinerants of the time make mention of the monastery of *"Panagia Gorgoepikoou"* which is believed to have stood in the same site. Further mention of this monastery was made by the Russian monk Ignatius of Smolensk, who it appears visited Thessaloniki in 1405.

North west (main) elevation of Panagouda church, Thessaloniki. The church was the centre, around which the Greek community of the town was concentrated during the period of the Ottoman rule.

6.19. Saint Athanasios

The church of *Saint Athanasios* is located north of and alongside Egnatia Street and southeast of the church of Aheropeitos.

This *timber-roofed* church is a later-date structure, built in 1818, possibly on the foundations of an earlier building. In fact, a gold-sealed imperial document, dated 1329 and carrying the signature of the Byzantine Emperor Andronicus III Paleologus — which is currently in the possession of the Saint Lavras Monastery in Agio Oros (Mount Athos) — makes mention of the *"metohi"* of *Agios Athanasios* in Thessaloniki, without however specifying whether or not it was an earlier church that stood on the same site as today's church. Nonetheless, the discovery of ancient ruins which lay strewn in the church's courtyard up until 1880 further reinforces the possibility.

The church and all its property was dedicated in 1569 to the *Vlatades Monastery* by a synodal decree which was signed by Ioasaf Argyropoulos, the metropolitan of Thessaloniki at that time. Documents to confirm this fact can be found in the monastery's archives. In fact, this issue became the subject of a series of disputes between the *Vlatades Monastery* and the *Metropolitan of Thessaloniki* which lasted for centuries. The Patriarch Gabriel, in an effort to resolve the difficulties, became involved in the issue but to no effect.

The church was renovated and today is the parish church of the district.

South entrance (main) of St. Athanasios church Thessaloniki, with the inscription, "1818, 15th November".

6.20. Nea Panagia

The church of *"Nea"* or *"Megali Panagia"* is situated in the southeastern part of the old city, south of Tsimiski Str., and a short distance away from the sea and the *White Tower*.

It is a tile-roofed church which was built in 1727 to honour the memory of the Assumption of the Virgin Mary. This information is derived from the inscription on the marbel lintel over the church's southern entrance. Because the memory of the Assumption of the Virgin Mary is considered to be supreme to that of the *Birth* of the *Virgin* Mary, the church was given the name *"Megali Panagia"* in contrast to the *"Mikri Panagia"* also known as the church of *Panagouda*, where the Birth of the *Virgin* Mary is celebrated.

Various archaeological finds lead to the belief that during the Byzantine Period, there existed a monastery in the surrounding area of this church (12th century), which was built in honour of the Virgin Mary. In 1873 an inscription was found in the area which reads: *"This monastery of the Holy Mother of God (Theotokos) together with its dependant monasteries... of Monk Ioannis ςωλγ" (= 1325).*

Reference to the Monastery of the Virgin Mary is made by a seventeenth century priest and itinerant, R. de Dreux, who visited Thessaloniki in 1666. It is likely that the monastery was destroyed in 1690 by a fire.[

The south entrance to the church of Nea Panagia, Thessaloniki, distinguished for the variety of its morphological elements.

The frescoes of the church of Nea Panagia have great interest and consist a characteristic sample of this Art as it was developed in Thessaloniki (and the area around it) during the 19th century.

During the course of recent restorations to the church interesting wall structures were uncovered at the south, western and eastern sides of the church. Various marble sculptures found enclosed within the walls as well as marble parts of porticoes belonging to an earlier building can leave no room for doubt that the further study of this monument and the topography of the area will bring to light significant findings concerning the history of both the monument and the city in general.

1.

2.

1. Inscription, over the south entrance of Nea Panagia church, Thessaloniki. Here it is mentioned that the building was erected during the year 1727.
2. Sample of the masonry from Nea Panagia church with incised marble stones coming from an earlier building.
3. Virgin Mary and Christ. Wall painting from the church of Nea Panagia.
4. Hierarchs. Wall painting from the church of Nea Panagia.

3.

4.

6.21. Saint Antonios

The church of *St. Antonios* is located in the eastern section of the *old city* at the corner of D. Margariti and Filikis Eterias Streets, a short distance away from the *Hippodrome*, which during the time of the Turkish Occupation was considered to be the "nucleus" of Hellenism.

The church of *St. Antonios* is a later-date building which was built during the second half of the nineteenth century. It is a typical tile-roofed, two-aisled basilica with an arcade which is no longer in existence today. This small church was part of a group of other buildings and was dependant on the earlier church of *Saint Constantine* which was situated in the present day Hippodromiou Square. The church of Saint Constantine was demolished and a new church was built in its place. The eastern side of *Saint Antonios* was supported by the fortified wall which once existed in the area but which was later demolished. Certain indications point to the existence of an ancient structure, possibly a chapel, which was located on the same site and was used as a place of worship.

According to Christian tradition, *St. Antonios* was the patron saint of the insane. In fact, iron rings that were found in the church seem to have been used to restrain the insane who it was hoped would be cured by the divine grace of Saint Antonios.

North west elevation of St. Antonios church, Thessaloniki. This church was once dependant to the church of St. Constantine in Hippodromiou square.

7. Moslem Monuments of Thessaloniki

Today, there still remains a large number of important *Moslem monuments* and *buildings* that were constructed during the Turkish Occupation. Many of these buildings which were located in the city's centre, were completely destroyed in the fire of 1917. Those that have survived to the present day are stone or brick stuctures.

According to historical references, in 1430, when the Turks captured the city, they took over these Greek edifices which they mainly used to serve administrative, military and religious purposes, as well as to accomodate their housing needs. The most significant and grandest of Byzantine churches were converted into Moslem mosques (*dzamia*) next to which tall *"minarets"* were built and stood as symbols of the conqueror's arrogance and superiority over the "faithless" subjugated Greeks. It wasn't until much later, when the Balkan peninsula became politically stabilized and the administration of the occupied territories organized, that Muslim structures began to be erected by Greek construction co-operations, that persisted in keeping the Byzantine tradition alive even through these buildings, during the whole period of Turkish oppression.

A very typical example of Byzantine building methods is the *"Bezesteni"* or roofed market place, located at the Egnatia and Venizelou streets intersection, which dates back to the first century of the Turkish Occupation.

The above mentioned streets (Egnatia and Venizelou) have been situated in the exact same position since ancient times and seem to have always been a part of the city's commercial district. Slightly northeast lies the city's Ancient Market place (Agora). The *"Bezesteni"*, which was considered by 16th century itinerants to be the most beautiful market place in the whole Balkan area, housed the shops of a variety of merchants but was principally made up of drapers' and jewellers' shops. Indeed, it was a well organized unity, which functioned according to a set of union regulations.

Of the *Moslem mosques (dzamia)* which were built for the purpose of praying, the following have been preserved:

— The *"Hamzà-Bèy dzami"* which is now the *"Alkazar"* at the Egnatia and Venizelou Streets intersection, which is believed to have been built in 1468.

— The *"Alatzà Imarèt dzami"* situated on a side street of Kassandrou Str., which was built by Isaàk-Pashà in 1500. This multi-domed structure stands out from the rest because of its multi-coloured minaret, constructed with colourful tiles, part of which still stands today.

— The *"Yenì dzami"* on Archaeological Museum Str. in the eastern part of the city, which was built in 1902, as a mosque for *"donmedes"* (converted Jews), based on the plans of the Italian architect *Vitaliano Poselli*.

— The *"Saatli dzami"* which was located next to the *Government Administration Building ("Diikitirio")* where the French and German consuls were slain by the Turks in 1876.

— The *"Bourmali dzami"* with its spiral minaret which was situated on Egnatia Str. near Democratias, (Vardari) Square, and the *"Pismanijè dzami"* west of the church of St. Dimitrius were all destroyed in the Big Fire of 1917.

The following Turkish *bath houses ("hamàm")* have survived up to the present day and have until recently been in use.

— The *"Yaountì Hamàm"* on Frangini and Vasileos Herakliou Streets.

— The *"Hamàm Bèy"* (currently the *Paradise Bath House*) possibly built in 1430 by Mourad II located on Egnatia Str., very close to the big Market Place called *"tsarsi"* which existed during the Turkish Occupation.

— The *"Pashà Hamàm"* (currently the *Phoenix* Bath House) at the P. Karatza and Kalvou streets intersection and which lies southeast of the Holy Apostles Church.

— The *"Yenì Hamàm"*, located at the Kassandrou and Saint Nikolaou streets intersection and north of the church of St. Dimitrius, which was possibly built on Roman ruins.

Furthermore, a number of Turkish drinking *fountains* located in the *Ano Poli* district and a Turkish tomb called *"turbès"* which is located in Terpsitheas Square have also been preserved.

Finally, one of the most characteristic examples of the Turks' attempt to embellish the city is the old *Syntrivani (Old Fountain)* which was built at the end of Egnatia Str. and from which the Square received its name. This monument, which has recently been restored by the city's authorities, was constructed in 1866 to dispel the bad impression that had been created to the city's people when, during the same period, the Turks demolished the district's byzantine fortified wall, so that they could build the Avenue then called *"Hamidiè"*.

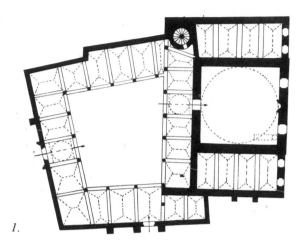

1. Plan of Hamza-Bey Dzami on Egnatia Str. (built 1468).
2. Southeast elevation of Hamza-Bey Dzami.

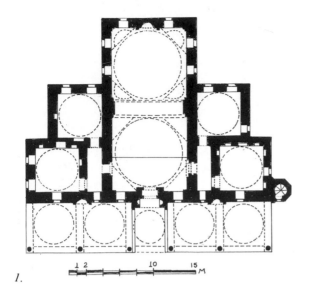

1.

1. Plan of Aladza - Imaret Dzami. The building was probably erected around 1500 by Isaak Pasha.
2. South west elevation of the "multi-domed" Aladza Imaret Dzami, Thessaloniki. The base of the colourful minaret can still be seen on the west side of this picture.

2.

1.

1. Gas street lamps from Yeni-Dzami, Thessaloniki.
2. Northwest (main) elevation of Yeni Dzami, Thessaloniki. This building was constructed in 1902 according to the plans of the Italian architect Vitaliano Pozelli as a temple of the "Donmeds".

2.

1. Bezesteni, the covered market have been at the intersection of Egnatia and Venizelou strs., Thessaloniki. This building is considered to be built during the first century of the Ottoman rule, in order to house various merchants (mainly drapers and goldsmiths).

2. Yahoudi Hamam at the intersection of Vas. Herakleou and Frangon strs., Thessaloniki.

The old fountain of the Fountain (= Syntrivani) square, in Thessaloniki. Sabri-Pasha demolished in 1869 the waterfront part of the Byzantine walls of the city and later in 1889 Midat Pasha demolished the eastern part of the walls. On the axis of the eastern walls, a new street was created, named Hamidiè Avenue. But a bad impression was created to the people of the city, and mainly the Greeks, so the Turkish government of the city decided to embelish that area by constructing a fountain, which, apart from its decorative function, was also used for the watering of the animals. The inauguration of the fountain was done with grandeur, as it is shown in this picture.

This fountain was restored and placed in its original site in 1977 by the municipality of Thessaloniki according to plans made by the author and with his supervision.

C´ Popular Arcitecture and Neo-Classical Structures

Apart from the more recognized monuments of Thessaloniki (Hellenistic, Roman, Byzantine etc.) the city also possesses a large display of individual structures as well as entire housing blocks which belong to the Modern Period of Architecture (*Popular Architecture and Neo-classical Structures*).

The big fire which in 1917 devastated the *"historical"* centre of Thessaloniki (burnt zone) also destroyed the general lay-out plan of the city. Hundreds of *"traditional"* buildings situated in the old part of the city as well as unique monuments were destroyed before a conclusive study of them could be recorded.

From the old city, the section of the *Ano Poli* which lies within the Byzantine walls and Athenas Str. (Olympiadas) was partially saved from the fire. In the *"Exohes"* district of the eastern section, which mainly began to develop in the second half of the nineteenth century, very few mansions (*"arhontospita"* or *"pyrgi"*) have survived to the present day. The same is true of the *"burnt zone"* of Thessaloniki. After the big fire the city's new street-plan was undertaken by a team of engineers headed by the French architect and city-planner *Ernest Hébrard.* A number of structures were later built to whose architecture the principles of *"eclecticism"* were applied.

Master plan of Thessaloniki in 1923.

120

The section of the *Ano Poli* which escaped destruction in 1917 is situated at the highest northernmost part of the old city. It covers an area beginning from the northern side of Saint Dimitriou Str. continues northwards up to the Acropolis wall and is bordered on the west and east sides by the Byzantine walls which have remained almost intact.

Despite the fact that this district has not been excavated by archaeologists there is little doubt that it remained for the most part uninhabited: "Hellenistic", "Roman" and "Byzantine" periods. It was established as a residential area during the Turkish Occupation and during the last years of the nineteenth century it became even more thickly populated mainly because of its good climate and the splendid view which it commands.

This area includes important monuments of Thessaloniki: The walls and the *Acropolis* itself with the *"Heptapyrgion"* (the seven towers), the church of *Osios David* (*Latomos Monastery*), the church of *St. Nikolaos Orphanos*, the church of *Taxiarhes*, the *Vlatades Monastery, St. Catherine's* church, the church of the *Prophet Elias*, a public bathhouse built during the *Byzantine period* which is located in Krispou Square, the *Alatzà Imarèt* which is on Kassandrou St. and many more.

Apart from these monuments, whole sections of the original city plan have remained unchanged in the *Ano Poli* district. It is a quaint district having narrow cobblestone streets, cul-de-sacs, small clearings and squares. But above all, it has buildings of *Popular Macedonian architecture* whose

The area of the Ano Poli of Thessaloniki.

121

plain style and functional purpose are unsurpassed. These buildings which are of a simple and unpretentious style mainly populate the districts surrounding the churches of Taxiarhes, Osios David, Vlatades Monastery and the streets of Dimitriou Poliorkitou, Alexandrou Papadopoulou, Theophilou, Antiochou, Amphetrionos, Herodotou, Tsamadou and Sahtouri.

Although built of simple and base materials they nevertheless are impressive buildings owing not only to their appearance but also to their interior functionalistic purpose. A typical feature is their simple architectural style that includes elements borrowed from the Ancient Greek and Byzantine traditions. Such elements are the bay-windows (*"sahnisià"*, the byzantine *"heliako"*) and the roofed balconies (*"hayàtia"*) which are also typical features of *Greek Popular Macedonian Architecture.*

A typical house of the Ano Poli of Thessaloniki on Alex. Papadopoulou str. (painting by M. Zaferiadis). The "sahnisi", in the first floor which was called by the Byzantines "Heliako", is a dominant morphological and functional element in the architecture of this area's building.

1.

1. House on Sahtouri Str. in the Ano Poli of Thessaloniki with successive "sahnisi" (bay windows) along its front elevation.
2. House on Theophilos Str. in Ano Poli of Thessaloniki (painting by M. Zaferiadis).

2.

House of Dimitrius Poliorkitis str. in Ano Poli of Thessaloniki.

House of Dimitrius Poliorkitis str. in Ano
Poli of Thessaloniki. Detail from a bay
window (sahnisi) on the first floor.

Until the middle of the nineteenth century when the Greek Revolution (1821) upset Turkish rule, Thessaloniki was mostly confined to the "fortified" area and very few buildings existed beyond these limits. However, from the second half of the nineteenth century onwards, this situation began to change as, with the formation of the first independent Balkan state in southern Greece, relative peace was restored. At the same time great efforts were made to improve the Turkish administration particularly in the occupied Balkan areas. Furthermore, the development of capitalistic production relations, the commercialization of the market, and the creation of two new classes (the merchant middle-class and that of the public administration's high officials) gave rise to the need for expanding the city's limits, especially to the eastern district (*"Exohes"*) where the first magnificent mansions (*"pyrgi"*) were built by well-to-do Greeks, Turks, Jews, Donmedes (converted Jews), Francs and Levantines.

Along Vasileos Georgiou and Vasilisis Olgas Streets as well as in the centre of Thessaloniki, magnificent edifices were constructed on big plots of land. Many of their architectural elements were of a *Neoclassical style* and a variety of their decorative motifs were influenced by the mood and spirit of *Art Nouveau* and *Romanticism*. Although these buildings did not belong to any clearly defined style of architecture, their heavily decorated pediments and cornices illustrated a return to ancient *Greek prototypes* (especially of the *Doric style*) as well as a tendency to borrow foreign elements whose aesthetic principles were influenced by the Romantic Movement in Europe during the nineteenth century and the beginning of the twentieth.

Very few of these structures have survived to the present day. Among those that have, are:

The *"Diikitirio"*, the old Customs office, the former *"Dimotiko"* Hospital, the school of *Philosophy* of the university, the building of the *3rd Army Corps*, the *Ottoman Bank* (on Frangou and Leontos Sofou strs.), the former *5th High School*, the *Papafi* Orphanage, the *Allatini Villa* (where the sultan Abdul Hamit was imprisoned), the *Osmàn Ali Bèy* mansion, (the present day *"Melissa"* Orphanage), the mansion of the Division Commander *Seifoulah* (at the 25th March and V. Olgas strs. intersection), the present day *School for the Blind*, the *"Fernandes"* mansion (*casa Bianca*, at the intersection of Sofouli, and V. Olgas streets) etc. *Those buildings which have survived to the present day not only reflect the spirit and mood of the period they were built in but through their technique illustrate the centuries - old experience of the Greek who built them.*

1.

1. Diikitirion (Ministry of Northern Greece), of Thessaloniki in Diikitiriou square. The building was erected in 1891 according to the plans of the Italian architect Vitaliano Poselli on the site where once stood the Turkish "konaki".
2. The building of the old Custom office at the harbour of Thessaloniki. It was built in 1909 according to Freyssent's plans and is a typical example of reinforced concrete structure of the beginning of the 20th century.

2.

126

The former Dimotiko (municipal) Hospital "St. Dimitrius", one of the typical buildings from the beginning of the century, in Thessaloniki. It was used as a hospital of the city's greek community during the last years of the Ottoman rule.

1. The main building of the University of Thessaloniki, today the School of Philosophy. It is one of the most characteristic buildings of 19th's century last decade. It was built in 1887 according to the plans of the Italian architect Vitaliano Poselli and was originally used as a public Preparatory School (Idadié).

2. The building of the 3rd Army Corps, also a work of the Italian architect Vitaliano Poselli (1890) which was used originally as army barracks by the Turks.

The building of the old General Greek Consulate in Thessaloniki (during the period of the Ottoman rule) at the intersection of Agias Sophias and Proxenou Koromila strs. This building, which today houses the Museum of the "Macedonian Struggle", was erected on expenses of the national benefactor Andreas Syngros and according to the plans of the architect Ernst Ziller, right after the big fire of the year 1890. The General Greek Consulate in Thessaloniki, especially during the period of the Consul's Lambros Koromilas service, was the centre from where the whole Macedonian struggle was organized and coordinated, (1904-1908).

1. The Allatini Villa, in the old area of "exohes", in Thessaloniki, where once the Sultan Abdoul Hamit II was imprisoned after the revolution of the Neoturks (1909). The same building, right after the liberation of the city was used to house the newly founded University of Thessaloniki (1926). This building was built in 1896 according to the plans of the Italian architect Vitaliano Poselli.

2. The Papafi Orphanage (on Papafi Str.) is one of the typical neoclassical buildings of Thessaloniki. It was founded in 1894 with expenses of the Thessalonian benefactor Ioannis Papafis. It is a work of the architect Xenophon Peonidis.

1. Neoclassical building at the intersection of Vas. Olgas and 25th March strs. It was built in 1905 according to the plans of the architect Xenophon Peonidis as a residence of the Turkish Lieutenant General Seifoulah Pasha. It is today a property of the municipality of Thessaloniki.

2. Neoclassical building at the intersection of Vas. Olgas and Sofouli Strs. It was built in the beginning of the century by the Levantin architect Piero Arrigoni as a residence of the merchant Fernandez and was named "Casa Bianca". It is one of the most typical neoclassical buildings of Thessaloniki.

Neoclassical building on 105, Vas. Olgas Str. It was built in 1893 according to the plans of Piero Arrigoni as a residence of the wealthy Turk-Albanian merchant Mehmet Kapandzi.

1. Typical bourgeois residence of old Thessaloniki (34, Evzonon Str.). The building has pronounced baroque elements, and its dominant feature is the rounded pediment containing relief representations of giants' battle. It has also a niche on its central axis with a statue in. It was built in 1920 as a residence of the fighter of the "Macedonian Struggle", K. Mittas.

2. Detail from the niche with a statue in from the house on 34, Evzonon str.

The historical building of the 5th Boys' High School in Thessaloniki (on 108, Vas. Olgas str.). It was built in 1897 by the "donmé" Ahmet Kapandzi. It was used after the liberation of the city, as the seat of the Greek Army Commander (1912).

D´ Preservation Orders for the Monuments of Thessaloniki

The monuments listed below are preserved and protected by the following acts of Government due to their historical or traditional value:

1.	The Church of St. Athanasios	*ΦΕΚ 382/29-8-63 vol. II
2.	The Church of St. Catherine	ΦΕΚ 190/2-6-32 vol. II
3.	Acropolis-Heptapyrgion	ΦΕΚ 36/3-2-62 vol. II
4.	Alatzà Imarèt Dzami	ΦΕΚ 191/11-6-26
5.	The Church of St. Antonios	
6.	The Church of Aheropeitos	ΦΕΚ 36/3-2-62 vol. II
7.	Yeni Hamàm	ΦΕΚ 18/20-1-38
8.	The Church of Osios David	ΦΕΚ 203/22-9-27
9.	The Church of St. Dimitrius	ΦΕΚ 36/3-2-62 vol. II
10.	The Church of the Prophet Elias	ΦΕΚ 191/11-6-62 vol. II
11.	The Cistern and the Propylo of the Church of the Holy Apostles	ΦΕΚ 190/2-6-62
12.	Yahounti Hamam	ΦΕΚ 18/20-1-38
13.	The Byzantine Bathhouse of Ano Poli	ΦΕΚ 47/28-2-52 vol. II
14.	The Church of the Transfiguration of the Saviour	ΦΕΚ 191/11-6-26
15.	The Church of St. Minas	ΦΕΚ 382/29-8-63 vol. II
16.	The Metropolis	
17.	The Church of St. Nikolaos Orphanos	ΦΕΚ 191/11-6-26
18.	The Monastery of Vlatades	ΦΕΚ 191/11-6-26
19.	Yenì Dzami	ΦΕΚ 18/20-1-38
20.	Bezestèni	ΦΕΚ 36/3-2-62 vol. II
21.	Hamàm Bèy	ΦΕΚ 18/20-1-38
22.	The Church of Panagia Lagoudiani	ΦΕΚ 382/29-8-63 vol. II
23.	The Church of Nea Panagia	ΦΕΚ 382/29-8-63 vol. II
24.	The Church of Panagia Halkeon	ΦΕΚ 190/2-6-62 vol. II
25.	The Church of Panagouda	ΦΕΚ 382/29-8-63 vol. II
26.	The Church of St. Panteleimon	ΦΕΚ 190/2-6-62 vol. II
27.	Pashà Hamàm	ΦΕΚ 18/20-1-38
28.	Agiasma of Prodrome - Nympheu	ΦΕΚ 36/3-2-62 vol. II
29.	Greek Consulate	ΦΕΚ 165/23-4-60 vol. II
30.	The Church of St. George, Rotonda	ΦΕΚ 36/3-2-62 vol. II
31.	The Church of St. Sophia	ΦΕΚ 36/3-2-62 vol. II
32.	The Church of Taxiarhes	ΦΕΚ 191/11-6-26
33.	The Fortified Walls	ΦΕΚ 36/3-2-62 vol. II
34.	The Church of Ypapanti	ΦΕΚ 382/29-8-63 vol. II
35.	Hamzà-Bèy Dzami	ΦΕΚ 191/11-6-26

Later-Day Monuments
(decisions made by the Ministries)

1. The Building at 105 Vasilissis Olgas Str.
   (The former NATO building) Y.A. A/Φ31/23549/3080/16-6-77

---

* ΦΕΚ: These acts of Government have been published in the Government Gazette.

2. The Allatini Villa
(at the corner of Vas. Olgas and Ploutonos Strs.)   Y.A. A/Φ31/23549/3080/16-6-77
3. The Ottoman Bank
(at the corner of Fragkon and L. Sophou Strs.   Y.A. A/Φ31/23549/3080/16-6-77
4. The "Melissa" Orphanage on Vasilissis Olgas Str   Y.A. A/Φ31/23549/3080/16-6-77
5. The 7th High School for Boys
in the Upper Town (Ano Poli)   .   Y.A. A/Φ31/23549/3080/16-6-77
6. The Italian Consulate on Vasilissis Olgas Str.   Y.A. A/Φ31/23549/3080/16-6-77
7. The Papafi Orphanage on Papafi Str.   Y.A. A/Φ31/23549/3080/16-6-77
8. The Old Customs Office at the harbour   Y.A. A/Φ31/23549/3080/16-6-77
9. The 1st High School for Boys
(at the corner of Vas. Georgiou and
Agias Triados Strs.)   Y.A. A/Φ31/23549/3080/16-6-77
10. The Annexe of the 1st High School for Boys   Y.A. 1485/40886/15-6-77
11. The 3rd Army Corps' building   Y.A. A/Φ31/23549/3080/16-6-77
12. The Seïfoulah Villa (the former IKA building)   Y.A. A/Φ31/27115/2956/24-5-76
13. The 5th High School for Boys
(on Vasilissis Olgas Str.)   Y.A. A/Φ31/27115/2956/24-5-76
14. Residence at 34 Evzonon Str.   Y.A. A/Φ31/27115/2956/24-5-76
15. Casa Bianca
(at the corner of Vasilissis Olgas and Sofouli Strs.) Y.A. A/Φ31/53186/4639/14-10-76
16. The Greek Consulate   N.Δ. 14418/865/28-3-60/
                                                     ΦΕΚ 165 vol. II
17. Residence at 14 Herodotou St. in the Ano Poli   Y.A. A/Φ31/61112/6995/15-1-77
18. 40 Residences in the Ano Poli district   Y.A. ΥΠΠΕ/ΓΔΠΑ/ΔΙΛΑΠ/Γ/
                                                     1483/40983/1-6-79/ΦΕΚ 680 vol. II
19. 8 Residences in the fortified wall district   Y.A. ΥΠΠΕ/ΓΔΠΑ/ΔΙΛΑΠ/Γ/
                                                     1483/40983/15-6-79/ΦΕΚ 680 vol. II
20. The Old Didaskalion (High School)on
Egnatia Str.   Y.A. 37881/1672/4-2-80
21. The School for the Blind
(located on Vasilissis Olgas Str.)   Y.A. 2784/68035/4-2-80
22. The Malakopi Arcade   Y.A. 2773/7163/4-2-80
23. Mihaëlidis Residence
(located on Vasilissis Olgas Str.)   Y.A. 2773/67036/5-2-80
24. The Sacre-study of Lazarists   Y.A. Γ/45816/991/1-8-80
25. The Saoul Modiano Arcade   Y.A. 995/43618/25-7-80
26. The Macedonian Museum of
Folklore and Ethnology   Y.A. ΥΠΠΕ/2549/71324/
                                                     25-11-80
27. The Building at the corner of Vilara
and 3 Katholikon Strs.   Y.A. ΥΠΠΕ/1093/39790/4-7-80
28. The Building at the corner of Agias
Sophias and Tsimiski Strs.   Y.A. 72049/2666/19-2-81
29. The Building at 3 Vasileos Herakliou Str.   Y.A. Γ/445/16368/ΦΕΚ 119 B΄/
                                                     26-2-81
30. Building at 109 Egnatia Str.   Y.A. Γ/2890/5018/26-1-81

Basic Bibliography.

Αδαμαντίου Α., «*Η Βυζαντινή Θεσσαλονίκη*», Αθήνα 1914.

«*Αρχαιολογικόν Δελτίον*», διάφοροι τόμοι.

Βακαλόπουλου Α., «*Ιστορία της Θεσσαλονίκης, 315 π.Χ.-1912*», Θεσσαλονίκη 1947.

Βακαλόπουλου Α., «*Ιστορία της Μακεδονίας 1354-1833*», Θεσσαλονίκη 1969.

Beaujour F., «*Tableau du commerce de la Grèce*», τομ. 1-2, Paris 1800.

Vickers M., «*The Byzantine sea walls of Thessaloniki*», περ. «*Balkan Studies*» τ.2/1970.

Γούναρη Γ., «*Τα τείχη της Θεσσαλονίκης*», Θεσσαλονίκη 1976.

Cousinèry M.E.M., «*Voyage dans la Macedoine*», Paris 1831.

De Dreux Robert, «*Voyage en Turquie et en Gréce*», Paris 1925.

Δήμιτσα Μ., «*Η Μακεδονία εν λίθοις φθεγγομένοις και μνημείοις σωζομένοις*», τομ. 1-2, Αθήνα 1896.

Diehl Ch.-M. Le Tourneau-H. Saladin, «*Les Monuments Chrétiens de Salonique*», Paris 1918.

Diehl Ch., «*Salonique*», Paris 1920.

Dyggve E., «*Recherches sur le palais imperial de Thessalonique*», Copenhagen 1945.

Εκδοτική Αθηνών, «*Μακεδονία*», Αθήνα 1982.

Ευαγγελίδη Δ., «*Η Παναγία των Χαλκέων*», Θεσσαλονίκη 1954.

Θεοχαρίδη Γ., «*Ο ναός των Ασωμάτων και η Rotonda του αγίου Γεωργίου Θεσσαλονίκης*», Θεσσαλονίκη 1954.

Θεοχαρίδη Γ., «*Η Νέα Μονή Θεσσαλονίκης*», Θεσσαλονίκη 1955.

Θεοχαρίδη Γ., «*Τοπογραφία και πολιτική ιστορία της Θεσσαλονίκης κατά τον ΙΔ´ αιώνα*», Θεσσαλονίκη 1959.

Θεοχαρίδη Γ., «*Οι ιδρυταί της εν Θεσσαλονίκη μονής των Βλαττάδων*», Θεσσαλονίκη 1960.

Kiel M., «Notes on the history of some Turkish monuments in Thessaloniki and their founders», περ. «*Balkan Studies*» τ. 1/1970.

Kinch K.F., «*L'arc de triomphe de Salonique*», Paris 1890.

Κολώνα Β.-Παπαματθαιάκη Λ., «*Ο Αρχιτέκτονας Vitalliano Poselli*», Θεσσαλονίκη 1980.

Λάσκαρη Μ., «*Ναοί και Μοναί Θεσσαλονίκης το 1405 εις το Οδοιπορικόν του εκ Σμόλενσκ Ιγνατίου*», Θεσσαλονίκη 1952.

Λέτσα Α.Ν., «*Ιστορία της Θεσσαλονίκης*», Θεσσαλονίκη 1961.

Μακαρόνα Χ.Ι., «*Η Καμάρα, το θριαμβικό τόξο του Γαλερίου στη Θεσσαλονίκη*», Θεσσαλονίκη 1969.

Μακεδονική Εταιρεία, «*Αρχοντόσπιτα της Θεσσαλονίκης*», Θεσσαλονίκη 1976.

Μαντοπούλου Θ.Σ., «*Ο παραθαλάσσιος ναός του Αγίου Δημητρίου στη Θεσσαλονίκη*», Θεσσαλονίκη 1980.

Μέρτζου Κ., «*Μνημεία Μακεδονικής ιστορίας*», Θεσσαλονίκη 1947.

Μοσκώφ Κ., «*Θεσσαλονίκη, τομή της μεταπρατικής πόλης*», Αθήνα 1979.

Μουτσόπουλου Ν., «*Θεσσαλονίκη 1900-1917*», Θεσσαλονίκη 1980.

Μπακιρτζή Χ.Ν., «*Η βασιλική του Αγίου Δημητρίου*», Θεσσαλονίκη 1972.

Μωραϊτόπουλου Γ., «*Τοπογραφία Θεσσαλονίκης*», Αθήνα 1883.

Νικονάνου Ν., «*Οι Άγιοι Απόστολοι Θεσσαλονίκης*», Θεσσαλονίκη 1972.

Νικονάνου Ν., «*Οι βυζαντινές εκκλησίες της Θεσσαλονίκης*», Θεσσαλονίκη 1980.

Ξυγγόπουλου Α., «*Ο ναός της Θεοτόκου των Χαλκέων*», Θεσσαλονίκη 1918.

Ξυγγόπουλου Α., «*Το καθολικόν της μονής του Λατόμου εν Θεσσαλονίκη και το εν αυτώ ψηφιδωτόν*», Αθήνα 1929.

Ξυγγόπουλου Α., «*Η βασιλική του Αγίου Δημητρίου Θεσσαλονίκης*», Θεσσαλονίκη 1946.

Ξυγγόπουλου Α., «*Συμβολαί εις την τοπογραφίαν της βυζαντινής Θεσσαλονίκης*», Θεσσαλονίκη 1940.

Ξυγγόπουλου Α., «*Τέσσαρες μικροί ναοί της Θεσσαλονίκης εκ των χρόνων των Παλαιολόγων*», Θεσσαλονίκη 1952.

Ξυγγόπουλου Α., «*Η ψηφιδωτή διακόσμησις του ναού των Αγίων Αποστόλων Θεσσαλονίκης*», Θεσσαλονίκη 1953.

Ξυγγόπουλου Α., «*Οι τοιχογραφίες του Αγίου Νικολάου Ορφανού Θεσσαλονίκης*», Αθήνα 1964.

Ξυγγόπουλου Α., «*Τα ψηφιδωτά του ναού του Αγίου Δημητρίου Θεσσαλονίκης*», Θεσσαλονίκη 1969.

Xyngopoulos A., «*Thessalonique et la peinture macédonienne*», Thessalonique 1955.

Παζαρά Θ., «*Η Ροτόντα του Αγίου Γεωργίου στη Θεσσαλονίκη*», Θεσσαλονίκη 1974.

Παπαγεωργίου Π., «*Η εν Θεσσαλονίκη μονή των Βλαταίων και τα μετόχια αυτής*», Byzantinische Zeitschrift 8 (1898).

Παπαγεωργίου Π., «*Μνημεία της εν Θεσσαλονίκη λατρείας του Αγίου Δημητρίου*», Leipzig 1908.

Παπαγεωργίου Π., «*Θεσσαλονίκης ιστορικά και αρχαιολογικά*», Αθήνα 1912.

Παπαγιαννόπουλου Α., «*Ιστορία της Θεσσαλονίκης*», Θεσσαλονίκη 1982.

Πελεκανίδη Σ., «*Παλαιοχριστιανικά μνημεία Θεσσαλονίκης, Αχειροποίητος-Μονή Λατόμου*», Θεσσαλονίκη 1949.

Πέτσα Φ., «*Χρονικά αρχαιολογικά 1968-1970*», Θεσσαλονίκη 1974.

Προβατάκη Θ., «*Τα ψηφιδωτά των βυζαντινών μνημείων της Θεσσαλονίκης*», Θεσσαλονίκη 1971.

Προβατάκη Θ., «*Ο Ναός της Υπαπαντής του Χριστού Θεσσαλονίκης*», Θεσσαλονίκη 1975.

Στογιόγλου Γ.Α., «*Η εν Θεσσαλονίκη Πατριαρχική Μονή των Βλατάδων*», Θεσσαλονίκη 1971.

Στογιόγλου Γ.Α., «*Ο εν Θεσσαλονίκη Ναός της Παναγούδας, εξ ανεκδότων πηγών (1757-1905)*», Θεσσαλονίκη 1975.

Σωτηρίου Γ., «*Χριστιανική και βυζαντινή αρχαιολογία*», Αθήνα 1942.

Σωτηρίου Γ., «*Η βασιλική του Αγίου Δημητρίου Θεσσαλονίκης*», Αθήνα 1952.

Τάτη Κ., «*Το μονύδριον του Σωτήρος Χριστού εν Θεσσαλονίκη*», Θεσσαλονίκη 1918.

Taffel T., «*De Thessalonica einsqueargo*», Berolin, 1839.

Tafrali O., «Sur la date de l'église et des mosaique de Saint Démétrius de Salonique», *Révue Archéologique*, 1909.

Tafrali O., «*Thessalonique au XIVe siècle*», Paris 1912.

Tafrali O., «*Topographie de Thessalonique*», Paris 1913.

Texier C.-R. Pullan, «*Byzantine Architecture*», London 1864.

Τσιγαρίδα Ε.-Λοβέρδου Κ.-Τσιγαρίδα, «*Κατάλογος Χριστιανικών Επιγραφών στα Μουσεία της Θεσσαλονίκης*», Θεσσαλονίκη 1979.

Τσιούμη-Μαυροπούλου Χ., «*Ο Άγιος Νικόλαος ο Ορφανός*», Θεσσαλονίκη 1970.

Τσιτουρίδου Α., «*Η Παναγία των Χαλκέων*», Θεσσαλονίκη 1975.

Υπουργείο Δημ. Έργων, «*Άνω πόλη Θεσσαλονίκης*», Θεσσαλονίκη 1979.

Χατζηϊωάννου Μ., «*Θερμαῖς, ήτοι περί Θεσσαλονίκης*», Θεσσαλονίκη 1881.

Χατζηϊωάννου Μ., «*Αστυγραφία Θεσσαλονίκης*», Θεσσαλονίκη 1881.

Printed by
John Rekos & Co
Thessaloniki - Greece.